World War Two

The Atlantic and Its Enemies
World War One
The Eastern Front, 1914–1917
Europe Transformed

World War Two

A Short History

NORMAN STONE

ALLEN LANE
an imprint of
PENGUIN BOOKS

ALLEN LANE

Published by the Penguin Group
Penguin Books Ltd, 80 Strand, London WC2R 0RL, England
Penguin Group (USA) Inc., 375 Hudson Street, New York, New York 10014, USA
Penguin Group (Canada), 90 Eglinton Avenue East, Suite 700, Toronto, Ontario,
Canada M4P 2Y3 (a division of Pearson Penguin Canada Inc.)
Penguin Ireland, 25 St Stephen's Green, Dublin 2, Ireland
(a division of Penguin Books Ltd)
Penguin Group (Australia), 707 Collins Street, Melbourne, Victoria 3008, Australia
(a division of Pearson Australia Group Pty Ltd)
Penguin Books India Pvt Ltd, 11 Community Centre,
Panchsheel Park, New Delhi – 110 017, India
Penguin Group (NZ), 67 Apollo Drive, Rosedale, Auckland 0632, New Zealand
(a division of Pearson New Zealand Ltd)
Penguin Books (South Africa) (Pty) Ltd, Block D, Rosebank Office Park,
181 Jan Smuts Avenue, Parktown North, Gauteng 2193, South Africa

Penguin Books Ltd, Registered Offices: 80 Strand, London WC2R 0RL, England

www.penguin.com

First published in the United States of America by Basic Books,
a member of the Perseus Books Group 2013
First published in Great Britain by Allen Lane 2013
001

Copyright © Norman Stone, 2013

Printed in Great Britain by Clays Ltd, St Ives plc

A CIP catalogue record for this book is available from the British Library

ISBN: 978-1-846-14139-3

www.greenpenguin.co.uk

ALWAYS LEARNING   **PEARSON**

Contents

List of Illustrations

List of Maps

Introduction

The Europe of 1914 looks very grand, if you judge it from the great monuments put up in any of the capitals of the time. There is a triumphalist air to them—The Mall in London, the imperial centre of a quarter of the world's land surface; the new Hofburg in Vienna, where everybody must have felt like an exhibit in the museum that the city was shortly to become; the Millennium monument in Budapest, celebrating the 1000th anniversary of the Hungarians' arrival in Central Europe; the enormous Victor Emmanuel wedding cake in Rome. Paris had had the Napoleonic treatment somewhat before, and the triumphalism of the period is shown mainly in the Pont Alexandre III. If you were European or American, you were supposed to be a master of the universe, and even the lesser capitals, such as Brussels (reigning over the Congo), had their pompous displays. The most spectacular of these is not in Europe but in the jewel in the British Crown, the city of New Delhi, designed by Sir Edwin Lutyens for a viceroy, Lord Curzon, who said in 1904 that the British should rule in India 'as if for ever'. They were in reality going to be out in 1947, and by then all these grand capitals were smashed or at least made very shabby by war. Berlin's centre was just rubble, and on the Siegesallee (Victory Avenue) the lumpish busts of the charmless rulers of Brandenburg glowered out over a waste of weeds, burnt shrubbery, and the corpses of animals that had escaped from the nearby zoo. The century had begun with the pomp and circumstance of Queen Victoria's funeral, when the rulers of the world had come to London, but it was not even halfway through when the whole imperial show had its own funeral, in 1945.

Only thirty years passed between the start of the First World War and the end of the Second and, with a brief interruption in the second half of the 1920's, they were calamitous. Until 1914, everyone, bar a few pessimistic writers, had believed in Progress. H. G. Wells had been its principal spokesman: science would save mankind. By 1945, in his final book, *Mind at the End of Its Tether*, Wells had turned blackly pessimistic. But it turned out that he was wrong again. After 1945, or at any rate after the Marshall Plan was launched in 1947, peace and prosperity reigned, and the thirty-year nightmare receded. The world, or at least the Western world, returned to an earlier pattern, that of the later nineteenth century. The last forty years of that century had seen the greatest economic quantum leap in modern history, if you consider the starting point. Horses and carts became motorcars; hospitals became places for recovery, not death through infection or pain; film, aircraft, psychoanalysis, skyscrapers, telephones—all products of that generation. Life expectancy shot up, and populations doubled. It is also true that the cultural life of the time was astonishing. For a natural scientist, the world of 1910 was miraculous. Without a passport, and without spending very much, you could go to international gatherings organized by a Belgian industrialist, Ernest Solvay, and discuss mathematics and physics with the most powerful brains in the world: Henri Poincaré, Albert Einstein, Marie Curie. In education, there had in most countries been reforms that made high schools better than today's universities. People knew their Bible and the national classics; the standard of musical performance was extraordinarily high; publications abounded, and serious writers such as Thomas Mann or composers such as Richard Strauss (they were both *very* careful with money) could become rich. But the writers' pessimistic cast of mind was justified, because the First World War emerged from it all, and then a Second World War soon emerged from that. Why?

The short answer is, of course, Germany. Otto von Bismarck's creation was the great success story, and her rulers lived in his shadow. Germans began to regard Slavs as inferior. Poles, by the millions, migrated west into Silesia or the industrial Ruhr, and took generations to assimilate. Prussian kings had had to learn Polish as a matter of course, and the first one to forbid his son to learn it was the nationalist-liberal father of Kaiser Wilhelm II. Prussia had generally had a very close relationship with Russia, the rulers of which were anyway either German or heavily influenced by Germans. But that changed in the 1890's, as Russia counted as backward and barbarous. She also took up a military alliance with France, Germany's rival, getting in return a large amount of French investments. By 1914 these were paying off. Russia was catching up fast, and there was wild alarm in

German military circles that in a two-front war they would be crushed. These alarms affected a wide area. There was Austria-Hungary, the Habsburg Empire, clearly in process of dissolution; and there was Ottoman Turkey, even more clearly in that process, and yet controlling both the oil of Iraq and the Bosphorus Straits, through which passed Russia's all-important grain trade and much else. When the straits were briefly closed in 1911–12 the economy of southern Russia nearly shut down as well. Germany and Russia were on a collision course over these matters.

The trouble was that Germany had made enemies besides Russia. The French had never really reconciled themselves to the defeat that they suffered at Bismarck's hands in 1870, and they made a huge effort at recovery—a large army (they even conscripted monks), an empire-building navy, and an ambitious foreign policy, directed at alliance with Russia. But French hostility would be containable, provided that the British remained neutral. And it was here that Germany, around the turn of the twentieth century, made her greatest mistake. She planned a navy, with a view to what was called *Weltpolitik*—'world policy', meaning empire. But the ships were not like British or French ones, which were meant to go round the world, defending overseas trade and possessions, and therefore needed coaling capacity, which in turn limited the weight that could be put into armour-plating. German ships were constructed with very limited coaling capacity, and so they could pile on weight in extra armour-plating. It took time for the British to realize that the German warships were really only intended to remain in European waters, and that they would be less vulnerable than the more thinly armoured British ones. And the whole point of the German navy was to bully or blackmail the British into granting imperial concessions to Germany—concessions in the first instance meant to be in China, but later on in the Middle East, the lands of the old Ottoman Empire. German ships, directed over the North Sea, spelled out the same sort of threat before 1914 as did Hitler's air force before 1939. Far from cowing the British, it caused them to take up alliances elsewhere. Alliance with Japan in 1902 lessened their weight of responsibilities in the Far East. In 1904 they took up a semi-alliance with France, the *Entente Cordiale* ('friendly agreement'). On the face of things, this was a colonial bargain involving North Africa. There had been rivalry over Egypt, where the British had established a protectorate and excluded the French. The French in turn had established themselves in Morocco and needed international support. Now, a deal was done: Morocco for France, Egypt for England. Behind the scenes, there were naval understandings—the British would take care of the North Sea, the French, of the Mediterranean. Later on, these agreements were extended, as the British did a deal with Russia and, after 1911, made plans for military assistance to France in the event of a German attack. Freud defines neurosis as that condition which realizes its own worst nightmares, and Germany was in such a state.

One of the most famous German books on World War One has the title *War of Illusions*. It is extraordinary to see how highly educated men confidently assumed as truth things that turned out to be grotesquely wrong. The list goes on and on—that empires enriched, that battleships were vital, that gold was credit, that blockading exports would cause revolutions, that fortresses would stop invasions, that morale would win battles. There was much talk of national honour, but as Falstaff says, 'What is honour? A word. What is in that word honour? What is that honour? Air.' In 1914 the Europeans' imperial world seemed to be falling apart, and there was a geopolitical tectonic shift, in that Russia, at last, was fulfilling her potential. Germany panicked, and her rulers made an effort to set up a sort of United Europe, ruled from Berlin, which would include the main components of a shattered Russia. The last great illusion was that the war would be short. When, at the Battle of the Marne on 9 September 1914 that proved wrong, the Europeans had an encounter with the reality of modern war. Before 1914, Europe had been beset by the twin problems of social conflict and imperialist nationalism. In 1917, both now emerged in force, with a Communist revolution in Russia and the intervention of the United States in the war, which would mean the end of European imperialism. The treaties that ended World War One were an uneasy compromise, and never had much validity, whether in morality or in force.

The treaty negotiated at Paris and signed at Versailles in June 1919, which ended the war, was also an exercise in illusion. As a Frenchman remarked, it was too soft for its harshness. The situation of 1919 was artificial. Germany and Russia were removed from the stage, and Great Britain and France seemed to lay down the law in Europe. With American support, they established new states to the east, and for that matter in the Middle East as well. There was a greater Poland, stretching far into what had been western Russia, with a population only two-thirds Polish, containing three million Jews, ten percent of the population. There were Czechoslovakia and Yugoslavia, multinational states the basis of which was French patronage of the dominant peoples, the Czechs and the Serbs. There was a greater Rumania, not unlike Poland as far as national composition was concerned. Stretching into Ottoman territory, new states were devised—an Iraq that was cobbled together from three varied Ottoman provinces, Kurdo-Turkmen Mosul, Shia Arab Basra, Sünni-Orthodox Baghdad; a Syria and a Lebanon that made sense only if taken together with Iraq, and not much otherwise; a Palestine, an Israel-to-come, where Zionists and Arabs were already clashing by 1926; a Saudi Arabia, religious fanaticism rampant. Looking back from 2012, more than a century after the Italians, invading Ottoman Libya in 1911, gave the signal for World War One, it is extraordinary to reflect that the only one of these states that has worked has been modern Turkey (you could, with some literary flourish, perhaps include Ireland, in so far as she, too, was a postwar creation). The 'self-determination of peoples' as enshrined by the Versailles settlement did not do at all well. Nor did the parliamentary government that was encouraged by the victors. Constitutions were solemnly drawn up, and elections were held (in 'the South-Western Caucasus Republic', which briefly appeared in northeastern Turkey, voters were invited to throw a stone into either of two tins, under the watchful eyes of the Turkish military). Germany acquired, through assembled professors and other worthies in Weimar, a constitution of impeccable democratic credentials—referenda, proportional representation, women's suffrage, federal states with their own elections and parliaments (the largest by far being Prussia). Parliamentary ways persisted uneasily until 1929, and then the world's economy started to collapse.

Why the Depression happened is the greatest question of the twentieth century. 'Capitalism', as we have to call it, had been a great success, giving the West the fatal illusions of superiority that brought about these 'gimcrack empires, spatch-cocked together' (Jack Gallagher's phrasing in the *New Cambridge Modern History*). Part of the formula for this success had been what the economist Joseph Schumpeter called 'creative destruction', the business cycle, where the lazy and self-indulgent went under, their assets being picked up cheaply by more energetic competitors. In the 1870's, Italian banks, for instance, were almost laughable, holding every transaction up to the light and advancing credit only gingerly: these sleepy banks were taken over by far-sighted German Jews, who invested long term in hydro-electricity. The takeover left much resentment among the losers. But in 1929 the process became one of destructive destruction— American money withdrawn from the system, the German mark collapsing, the English pound following, world trade dropping by two-thirds, and in France until 1938 what became known as 'negative growth'. This was a catastrophe, and present-day (2012) troubles are nothing in comparison, though the comparison is sometimes made. The United States had 25,000,000 unemployed, while Germany had 6,000,000—even then a misleading picture, in that unemployed German women were grossly undercounted. The problem was only solved through rearmament. Small wonder that a good proportion of the intelligentsia shifted to the Left. Still, the crisis was really the outcome of wartime debts, and more generally of the nervous, pessimistic atmosphere that the war had created. These, and the inexperience of the United States in managing its new role as a world power, went together with changes in technology that replaced men with machines. But the depression that followed was not really a terrible judgement on 'capitalism' as such; it was a consequence of the First World War.

And the Depression swept parliamentary governments away. Weimar Germany had always been weak, a fair-weather system, and democratic government depended on coalitions. A five-party one came up in 1929, and collapsed in March 1930 at the first signs of economic downturn: the right-wing liberals said that the unemployed should pay more for their insurance, and the moderate socialists said that the employers should pay more; disagreement over a quarter of one percent brought the government down, though of course there was more to it. No government then emerged with a majority in the Reichstag until Hitler came along in January 1933. In Austria, Poland, Rumania, and Greece, dictators and semi-dictators took over; Spain experienced a civil war that lasted from 1936 to 1939—her caudillo, Francisco Franco, proud about signing as many as 3,000 death warrants in the back of the car that took him every day from the Zarzuela Palace to his office in central Madrid. Only two countries east of the Rhine maintained civilized standards—Czechoslovakia, set up as a *Rechtsstaat,* a legal state, on the lines of the old liberal Habsburg monarchy, and conservative Hungary, where the standards of the old-fashioned aristocracy still prevailed. Mussolini had triumphed in 1922 in a sort of dress rehearsal for Thirties Fascism. In 1920, the Italian economy had collapsed, and there followed two years of near-anarchy. Italian Fascism grew out of the wartime officer corps, men who could only find a way forward in a sort of respectable protection racket, and that gave Hitler his model. It was also strikingly successful. By 1936, whatever the reason, German unemployment had dropped to a million, and though the country's standard of living was Spartan in comparison with the British, the economy was moving again and everyone noticed a new, assertive spirit (which most British people instinctively disliked).

But Adolf Hitler was really the result of a vacuum. That vacuum supplied him with arguments. The postwar settlement was supposed to be underwritten by a League of Nations in Geneva, but it was really only a matter of time before Germany once more asserted herself. The question would be: which Germany? A decent German state was needed, but the French especially did everything to undermine that—even, in 1931, refusing to cooperate with the British in keeping the German economy afloat. The list of vacuous failure goes on and on. Weimar democracy had turned into presidential rule-by-decree: the Reichstag had ceased to function. The Gold Standard, which was the symbol of the international financial and trading order, had become a deflationary weight, depressing everything except the self-importance of central bankers. The Germans had tied themselves to it, in part in order to pay off the reparations required by Versailles. It had become a prescription for mass unemployment. The

League of Nations, the Maginot Line, the Little Entente supposedly linking Czechoslovakia, Rumania, and Yugoslavia in a military alliance but not including Poland: all of them fictions, and
dangerous because bureaucracies were set up to maintain belief
in them. The first hundred-odd pages of A. J. P. Taylor's *Origins
of the Second World War* are the classic account of this. Of
course the inter-war period was hag-ridden by memories of the
Great War. France, especially, had been badly weakened, and
she was defending a shell. Louis-Ferdinand Céline's *Death on
the Installment Plan* spelled it out, dismal lives in some Rancy
or Eurcques-sur-Ourcqes housing estate: an embittered version
of George Orwell's *Coming Up for Air*. The problem was that
the western Powers conceded to Hitler what they had refused to
Gustav Stresemann, the liberal Weimar statesman who died in
1929. Hitler's idea was to bring about recovery in Germany by
gaining an empire in the east, to match the American and the
British hinterlands. He learned that, if he threatened to use force,
and claimed to have crushing armaments, the west would give
way, and maybe encourage him on his turn to the east. It was
there, at the expense of the despised Slavs, that Germany's empire would be built up.

And so it came to a Second World War, with a Hitler in
charge of German affairs. He had become very popular because
he had triumphantly cut through the web of hypocrisy and false-
hood that 'Versailles' represented. He had revived the German
economy; he was, for millions of Germans, a hypnotically powerful speaker; no longer were Germans humiliated and impov-
erished by a vengeful France. But in the course of this, he had

enraged the British in particular. In the summer of 1939, he thought that he could take over Polish territory without any British intervention. Then he got an unexpected deal with Stalin. The British could not now do anything for Poland; surely they would not even try. He miscalculated: there was a rebellion in the British political classes, and the ultimatum followed. Eventually, this too turned into a war of Great Britain, Russia, and the United States against Germany, a re-fighting, this time with even more destructive weaponry, and, through tanks and aircraft, a battlefield mobility going far beyond that of 1918. This war ended six years later, Central Europe in surreal ruins. There was a notice on the Dutch-German border reading, 'Here ends the civilized world.' But then at last matters improved: the German problem was solved, Germany became in many ways a model state, the Americans behaved with a sense of responsibility that they had refused to display in 1919, and the wars seem to belong to an unimaginable past.

Nineteen-forty-five marked the kind of moment when one era turns into another. Until then, European empires ran the globe, and my early school textbooks—already obsolete—informed me in 1950 about all the good the British had done in an India that, like a good quarter of the globe, was coloured British red. Winston Churchill, the grand aristocrat who had been born (in 1874) into the Victorian certainties, at that in a pre-electrical age (the first great house to be lit by electricity was Lord Salisbury's, Hatfield, in 1880), was counted as old-fashioned. The same was also true of his historic rival, Adolf

Hitler, but it was a different sort of old-fashionedness. He was born on the Austro-German border in 1889, and when he was in his teens, electricity, the miracle-working energy, was spreading, with endless new possibilities for building, transport, medicine, radio. Hitler later on was fascinated by machinery—more so than Churchill, who was mainly interested in the military aspects. In the Austro-German borderland, there was much resentment at the tyranny of the Catholic Church, which had once suppressed Protestants by main force, and Hitler grew up with an intense dislike for Christian morality—it moved him, and many others, far more than did anti-Semitism when he was a young man. That (according to Brigitte Hamann, a splendid historian who looked at the original evidence) he picked up later, and in his usual vindictive way persecuted an old Jewish couple who had been kind to him in the old days when he took refuge in their shop if, while he sold water colours to the tourists in Vienna, it rained. Adolf Hitler's species of nationalism—technology, Triumph of the Will, and elimination of the weak—was also old-fashioned by 1945. Hitler's version of the old Europe petered out in the black farce of his shelter, far beneath the Reichstag gardens, brilliantly captured in the German film *Downfall*. Churchill's also ended, with his final Prime Ministership in 1951, a mixture of mothballs and alcohol. In 1945, with the huge symbol of the atomic bomb, another world emerged.

Much later, as I got to know Germany and read her history, I stumbled upon people who had had a part in Hitler's war machine. I suppose the most extraordinary was Albert Speer. In 1981, I was doing a programme for BBC television about Hitler and art, and we asked Speer, Hitler's chief architect and the wartime minister of armaments, for an interview. Aged seventy-six, with a twenty-year prison sentence behind him, he agreed to come, much to our surprise. It was a holiday weekend, and in those days things in London shut down: I had to take him to the restaurant of Brown's hotel and he talked about the Third Reich. I was amazed that he did not know one of the most important facts about the Nazi vote, that Protestants were far more likely supporters than Catholics (Bavaria had her reputation, but owed it mainly to her Protestant third). I suppose religion just did not interest him. He also rather surprised me—I should not have been—in that he defended the British bombing of Germany's cities, on the grounds that it diverted much of the German effort away from the fighting fronts and for the defence of the homeland. It was somehow a massively sad evening, but we did our interview the following day, and he was good, though he must have said it all before. Then, full of beans, and admired by all the women there, he marched off to his hotel and died. Another of my odd connections with the Third Reich was with the son of Josef Mengele, the terrible doctor at Auschwitz who carried out genetic experiments on living souls and is said to have stood on the railway platform as the Jews tumbled out of the cattle cars, dividing those who could work from those who should just be sent straight to the gas chambers. He had left Auschwitz at the last moment with a box of eyeballs and tissue samples to show to his professor in Frankfurt, who of course panicked and showed him the door. Mengele died in Brazil in 1979, and the family went public with the story: I interviewed his son, a sympathetic and straightforward man who had been brought up by a decent social-democrat stepfather and was only told when sixteen who his real father was. He had flown to Brazil to see the man, and they had got on very badly—Mengele was a mean bore, living with a German refugee woman from Rumania with whom he quarrelled incessantly about small sums of money in inflatable Brazilian cruzeiros. He wrote a wooden novel about his escape from postwar Germany—if you reached Genoa via the Italian part of Tyrol, you got a Red Cross passport to the Argentine, where Mengele opened up for business under his own name. His son said that, when Mengele's university stripped him of his doctorate, there were protests from Auschwitz inmates who had been his associates, and this is just about believable. Eugenics, 'race research', was not just a Nazi specialty: in the progressive world of 1910, it concerned the Western world in general, and up to the 1970's Sweden was sterilizing Lapps, on the grounds that they were not worthy to breed. When you contemplate the talents of Speer and the purposes of Mengele, you can see what Churchill was after when he said, in 1940, that

> Hitler knows that he will have to break us in this island or lose the war. If we can stand up to him, all Europe may be free and the life of the world may move forward into broad, sunlit uplands. But if we fail, then the whole world, including the United States, including all that we have known and cared for, will sink into the abyss of a new Dark Age, made more sinister, and perhaps more protracted, by the lights of perverted science. Let us

therefore brace ourselves to our duties, and so bear ourselves that, if the British Empire and its Commonwealth last for a thousand years, men will say, 'This was their finest hour.'

It was not rational to resist in 1940, or for that matter to declare war in 1939, but Hitler did not cause people to react rationally. They knew in their bones that another great war was coming, and bright sparks in Great Britain knew that the best thing was to learn to fly, as did my own father, a budding lawyer at Glasgow University, in 1936. He took part in the Battle of Britain with the City of Glasgow 602 Squadron, but was then taken out of line to train pilots, of which there was desperate need. The historian Max Hastings says that the Royal Air Force, the RAF, did not have the personnel to maintain planes properly, and my father's went down over Wales in February 1942: I still have the compass. But it was a good world, and the officers put together a fund to look after my education at Glasgow Academy. I owe them a huge amount, and therefore dedicate this book to them.

WORLD WAR TWO

WORLD WAR TWO

chapter one | BETWEEN THE WARS

preceding page: Clemenceau, Wilson, and Lloyd George after
signing the Treaty of Versailles, June 1919 (Hulton-Deutsch
Collection/Corbis)

The end of World War One found Adolf Hitler, then a twenty-nine-year-old corporal, in an army hospital in northern Germany. He was recovering from a gassing that had temporarily blinded him, and news that Germany had been defeated came as a vast shock. She had fought the world for four and a half years, had come very close to victory, and still occupied much of western Europe and Russia. But in November 1918 there was a sudden collapse. Drunken sailors and brawling strikers ran riot, and the imperial government panicked, fled, and passed the cup to new rulers—the Left and its allies—who obtained an armistice on 11 November. Hitler wept, he said, bitter tears. The war should have been won, and it would have been won, he said, had it not been for the upper-class dimwits in charge, the treacherous Jews, the Left, and the sentimental academics who had undermined the war effort. Now, all was in vain. The troops had to go back to the Rhine and give up western Russia, where Communists were taking over.

It was not just Hitler who wept bitter tears, for the November armistice was not the end of the suffering. The British had imposed a blockade on Germany, and her towns were now starving. That blockade went on, and in Vienna children developed rickets, a disease of vitamin deficiency that leads to what the Germans call 'x-legs' or 'o-legs'—knock knees and bow legs. Then came an Allied occupation of the Rhineland—the zone west of the Rhine and the bridgeheads on the eastern banks—with the French in particular in no mood to forgive and forget. They now demanded a huge indemnity, given the hypocritical name 'reparations'. That sum came to 132,000 million gold marks, and the final payments (debts taken on in the 1920's to pay the original sums) would only be made in 2010. These payments were meant to shackle the German economy, to prevent rearmament or even just recovery.

Memories of the immediate postwar period embittered Central Europe for the next two decades. The victorious Allies had assembled in Paris in 1919 and drawn up peace treaties. The atmosphere, often described, was freakish. A moralizing American president, Woodrow Wilson, was set on a sort of new world order, and for a time he was lionized, surrounded by cheering crowds. America now had the money, and the Allies owed her enormous sums; she could shape the world much more than ever before. On the whole, she flunked the task, as she most notably did not do after the Second World War, when with the Marshall Plan, and much else she took a lead in promoting recovery, made dollars available for international trade, encouraged the Europeans to abandon their protectionist ways, and thus caused a wave of prosperity that the French called 'the thirty glorious years' (they came to an end with the oil shock and 'stagflation' of the mid-Seventies). The victors of 1918 look, in the official portrait, like a caricature-version Mount Rushmore of humbug and smugness, as they behold the enraged German delegate, Ulrich von Brockdorff-Rantzau, signing on the dotted line. The British had added millions of acres, especially in the once-Turkish Middle East, to their already vast empire and confiscated the German ships that menaced their trade. The French also took a slice of the Middle East and looked forward to receiving reparations money for generations to come. The Americans on the other hand were divided about being involved in the problems of the Old World. President Wilson had a vision, making sure the Great War was the war to end war. He preached democracy and national self-determination, but American democracy is tripartite and the Senate would not take responsibility for enforcing the treaty's terms. The Americans—or at least key Republican senators—would not even join the prototype United Nations, the League of Nations, that had specially been devised to give President Wilson a platform from which to moralize at everybody. A French general, seeing what was happening, said: 'This is a twenty years' armistice, not a peace treaty.' That man was right.

The most unstable element in the peace treaty was that it required German cooperation to enforce it. The Germans in November 1918 had done what they could to present themselves as a parliamentary and democratic state, to appeal for American sympathy. They got rid of the kaiser, and a republican constitution was adopted at Weimar in the February before the Versailles treaty was signed (in June 1919). It was a constitution of Germanic literal-mindedness—relentless voting at all levels, proportional representation, women's suffrage (which the French did not have), federal arrangements, provisions for a referendum to be staged if enough signatures were collected. Of course the resulting parliament, the Reichstag, was sometimes paralyzed if it had to deal with anything serious, and the president then ruled by decree. Coalitions wobbled and were discredited if they went too far in the direction of fulfilling the treaty. Eventually, the French recognized that they could not go on demanding the maximum reparations, the Americans stepped in with a loan to Germany, and for a few years there was what an American president, Wilson's successor, Warren Harding, referring to his own country, described as 'normalcy'.

Hitler had acquired a reputation throughout Germany in the early 1920s as a rabble-rouser of the Right. The army had used him as a spy in Munich, and he dropped in on the meeting of a small group called the National (meaning 'anti-foreign') Socialist (meaning 'stealing') German (meaning 'anti-Semitic') Workers (meaning 'lower-middle-class') Party. There he discovered his outstanding gift: he could speak in public. Generally, Germans were not good at it, for they lectured or ranted. Hitler was an accomplished mimic, an excellent actor, and used language in a way that was untranslatably funny (Sigmund Freud, Karl Kraus, Franz Werfel, also Austrians, and Franz Kafka, of Prague, had the same knack). He also hit upon anti-Semitism—a popular cause in some quarters, given that some Jews had survived economic trouble better than some other Germans and Austrians, were strongly represented in finance and the liberal media, and ran fashionable art galleries that promoted the sort of painting

6

that Hitler, who fancied himself an artist, abhorred. He spoke for a war of revenge, for a nationalist government that would just put an end to corrupt parliaments. His model was Italian: Benito Mussolini, a journalist who thought in headlines, set up a Fascist party (the name referred originally to anti-capitalist Sicilian peasant rebels in the late nineteenth century), and in 1922 took power. Germany was not ready for this in 1923, when Hitler also tried to take power—even the men of his old regiment distanced themselves. He had a few months' imprisonment, which he used to dictate a book, *Mein Kampf,* which laid out a diagnosis of and a programme for Germany. She must avoid the mistake of war on two fronts. Russia was the real enemy and that meant conquering living space *(Lebensraum),* raw materials, in the east. Communists were Jews, he wrote: they corrupted everything. In the good years of the Weimar Republic, he did not flourish, and the Bavarian bishops objected to the anti-Semitism on the grounds that it deterred tourists. Hitler was marginal and even comic.

Then in 1929 events began to move Hitler's way. That year the world financial crisis began, and it caused the fall of Germany's last real parliamentary government. Germans blamed foreigners for their plight and Jews for moving their money out. The mark came under pressure and ceased to be convertible. Travellers were searched at the frontier, and even a Princess Schönburg, travelling to London, had to go third-class for want of foreign exchange. Trade fell by two-thirds, and since Germany was dependent on exports, soon six million Germans were unemployed. In the 1932 federal election, thirty-seven percent of

Germans voted Nazi, twenty-two percent voted for the Social Democrats, and fourteen percent voted Communist. The Reichstag was powerless and only managed to find majority votes for dissolving itself (the only other yea vote, carried quite widely, was to deprive married women of security of tenure in the civil service). Berlin was in a murderous mess. In an atmosphere of bitterness and hatred, in January 1933, as the outcome of a deal with the conservatives, Hitler became chancellor.

The new chancellor's first important meeting was with the generals. He told them that he would rearm. Rearmament would give German industry something to do and absorb some of the unemployed. It was in defiance of the Versailles treaty, but Hitler calculated that the western Powers would not react. He had long been enthusiastic about aircraft and motorcars, the two foremost symbols of the ultramodern, and they translated easily enough into warplanes and tanks: he would soon boast of how many he had, and in reality exaggerated the numbers (which were then accepted in London and Paris). His generals meanwhile were thinking hard as to how the weapons might be used, and the lessons of 1918 came in at this point, for the British and French had won the last campaigns by combining tanks and aircraft. Rearmament went ahead, and the German air industry, for example, starting with only 3,000 employees making a few dozen planes, became a huge enterprise, by 1939 employing some 250,000, with a capacity to produce 3,000 warplanes a year. This upturn (and another in agriculture) was to give Germans full employment in 1936 again, and Hitler was hugely popular. There were of course signs of the horrors to come. In 1934,

Hitler had staged a violent coup against Nazi radicals, having them shot out of hand. Anti-Semitism was given legal backing in 1935. There were concentration camps with 6,000 inmates. But it was all quite limited, and many were still able to argue that, as Hitler became successful, his rule would become easier. That at any rate was a view taken in London especially. It was a view encouraged by the atmosphere at the most famous of all Olympic Games, those held in Berlin, in August 1936.

Far from getting kinder and gentler, however, the régime got harsher, extorted money from the Jews, and drove out hundreds of thousands of them. They lost two-thirds of their wealth when they left, and this paid for arms. In the summer of 1936, Hitler made the rearmament programme far more comprehensive, to prepare Germany for defensive war in four years, and aggressive war in seven. Part of Hitler's reasoning for this seven-year programme was that everything depended on him, and he felt he was very mortal: he was neurotic about his health. But the declared reason was that Soviet Russia was industrializing fast, with Stalin's Five-Year Plans: Hitler would compete and outdo the USSR. Here, he was gambling. Germany did not have the raw materials for an in-depth armaments drive, and she did not have the foreign exchange for the oil, the rubber, and the non-ferrous metals essential for aircraft and motorized warfare. A vast and expensive programme got under way for synthetic oil and rubber, and a huge metallurgical complex was set up under the Four-Year Plan organization of Hermann Goering, the chief of the Luftwaffe, the air force. The totalitarian character of the country was intensified, and the political police—Gestapo, for short—were fused in 1936 with the SS, the élite element in the Nazi Party, run by Heinrich Himmler.

In that summer of 1936, circumstances were right for a forward move by Hitler. The western Powers had become alienated from Italy. In the previous October, Mussolini, seeking empire, moved on Abyssinia, which had membership in the League of Nations, and he gained much hatred from high-minded British people in particular. Also in the summer of 1936, a civil war broke out in Spain, where a left-wing régime issuing from a questionable election was attacked, in a military coup that half-succeeded. The army leader, General Francisco Franco, paraded himself as a Fascist, and France, under a left-wing government, was supposed to stand by the Spanish Republic. She did not, but Mussolini intervened with soldiers and warships against it. The civil war lasted for three years and was exploited by Hitler, as an experimental ground for aerial bombing, and by Stalin, who was delighted to profit from the divisions of the western European Powers. He wanted the war to keep going, doled out arms for the Republic when it seemed to be losing and then stopped them when it seemed to be winning. When anarchists tried for a genuine revolution in Barcelona, he had them mown down by loyal Communists. The poisonous atmosphere of 1936 proved an ideal moment for Hitler to start his advance. In March German troops moved into the Rhineland, the area of Germany west of the river. The French had wanted to annex it, and had been refused. Instead, it was to be empty of troops and unfortified, so the French would not need to fear an invasion, whereas Germany was wide open to it. The British took a lead in stopping any French reaction in 1936. They intended to give Hitler much of what he wanted so as to deter him from forcing further issues: the policy known as 'appeasement'.

When Hitler re-militarized the Rhineland, however, the countdown to war began. And there was another countdown in the Far East, where the United States was directly involved. Japan had a history with curious European parallels: an island identity, like England, and a militaristic caste, like Prussia. She had been let down by the British when, after the war, an agreement was made as regards the size of navies in the Pacific. Then she faced discrimination against her trade when the world depression got going in 1930. The response of the militarists was to take over the industrial part of China, the northeastern area of Manchuria, which Japan invaded in 1931. She was then condemned by the League of Nations and found herself without allies. Hitler took an interest, because he wanted a counterweight to the Soviet Union, then considered his chief enemy and target. And so in November 1936, Germany and Japan signed an Anti-Comintern Pact, directed against the Communist International. Now Japan had friends in Europe, though for the moment the partnership did not have much to offer. Then in July 1937 an event occurred that sparked off the Far Eastern war. The Japanese army stood quite close to Peking (Beijing), and there was an incident at the Marco Polo Bridge that divided them from the Chinese. One of their soldiers went missing on the Chinese side; a standoff ensued; the Japanese then marched forward, easily defeating the Chinese Nationalists, who, though they had made strenuous efforts over the past ten years, were no match in weaponry or discipline. The whole situation was bedevilled again because there was a separate Chinese force, the Communists, who eventually established themselves at a stronghold in northwestern China, close to the Soviet border. The Nationalists had first cooperated with them and then turned against them; the Communist leader Mao Tse-tung escaped to the countryside, where he mobilized peasants. In all of this warring, China was wrecked, with epidemics and endless atrocities, the most famous of which occurred when the Japanese besieged the Nationalists' capital, Nanking (Nanjing), late in 1937. There was an orgy of raping and killing that disgusted all observers, who could not believe that the Japanese could behave in this way.

A complicated four-cornered struggle got under way in China: Nationalists versus Japanese; Nationalists versus Communists; Communists—not often—against Japanese; and in the summer of 1939, the Soviet Union, on the Manchurian border, versus Japanese. The Americans had given support to the Nationalists but were not anxious to be involved in the fighting; and Hitler's support for the Japanese was mainly verbal, though he did withdraw the German generals who were advising the Nationalists (they were prominent: Hans von Seeckt, who had reconstituted the German army in the 1920's, and Alexander von Falkenhausen, who became governor-general of Belgium). At any rate, here was a factor that could further complicate the relations of Germany with the rest of the world, and there were people who compared the vast conflict in China with the Civil War in Spain, a straightforward battle between Good and Evil. Japan began to get very negative press in the United States.

Meanwhile, in Europe, there was careful thinking behind the policy of appeasement. The grievances that had carried Hitler to power were genuine enough, and these could be redressed. There were millions of Germans in Poland and Czechoslovakia, and they had never wanted to be included in these countries. As for the six million Germans of Austria, their representatives in the Imperial parliament had voted to join Germany when the Austro-Hungarian Empire fell apart in 1918, and the only dissent came from a Catholic bishop who thought that Germany was too Protestant. The French had put a stop to that and for a time could not even find a name for the country. It was a Frenchman, Georges Clemenceau, who solved the problem saying, 'Austria is what's left.' Its independence had been unhappy, a Catholic peasant country with a socialist capital full of civil servants who had once governed an empire, and in 1934 there was a sort of civil war, in which army artillery bombarded working-class housing. When Hitler, born in Austria, and not a German citizen until 1932, proved successful in Germany, there was agitation for Austria to join Germany, and the local Nazis proved rowdy. Hitler adopted their cause, with raucous, bullying speeches at Nazi rallies where brown-shirt uniforms marched about, under a show of lights managed by Hitler's favoured architect, Albert Speer, who said that he owed the mesmerizing techniques to the Weimar cinema. To the government in London, it did not really make sense to force Germans to live in countries where they were second-class citizens. In November 1937 the British foreign secretary, Lord Halifax, went to Berlin and indicated to Hitler that the British would not oppose him if

he chose peaceful methods for an alteration of the postwar settlement. The British absolutely did not want war. Not only were
memories of the slaughter of 1916 well and truly alive, with war
memorials in any school or university that went on and on with
the reading of the names of the dead, but they were faced with
potential enemies in two hemispheres and, in India, rebellion
as well.

As Austria's Nazis became more and more restive, the Catholic
chancellor, Kurt von Schuschnigg, appealed to Hitler to control
them. He had already appointed Hitler's nominees to important
posts in his government. In February 1938 he travelled to
Hitler's retreat at Berchtesgaden and was there bullied by Hitler,
who brought on his most fearsome-looking generals and reduced
Schuschnigg to a nervous wreck by forbidding him to smoke.
Schuschnigg at first accepted Hitler's terms for cooperation—
they would have turned Austria into a satellite—and then, when
he went back to Vienna, he changed his mind, saying that he
would instead hold a plebiscite, which of course he would win.
His hope was that the west and Mussolini would save him.
Hitler gambled that they would not do so and on 14 March invaded Austria. No one did anything: on the contrary both the
cardinal and the one-time Socialist president, Karl Renner, wel-
comed the Nazis, as Austria was turned into a German province
and the quarter-million Jews of Vienna faced vile humiliations,
violence, and theft. Mussolini had protected Austria before.
Now he did nothing, and Hitler sobbed into the telephone to his
representative in Italy that he should tell Mussolini he would
never forget this, never, never—a promise that Hitler kept. With

Austria part of Germany, the pressure was now obvious on Czechoslovakia, which had a long and vulnerable frontier. Three million Germans lived in Czechoslovakia, mainly in the Sudeten area close to Germany, and Hitler drove them towards fever pitch. Czechoslovakia was famously the only democratic country east of the Rhine, and its population could vote. A majority among the Germans voted for a nationalist party.

In the summer of 1938, as Nazi tyranny spread over Vienna, and the Jews were pushed out, pressure mounted on Prague. Czechoslovakia was a creation of the postwar treaties, and it depended on a French alliance, which would come into effect if Germany attacked. The British again took the lead in ensuring that France did nothing. They absolutely did not want war for a country of which, the prime minister complained in a radio broadcast, they knew nothing and cared less. In September 1938 that elderly figure, Neville Chamberlain, brandishing an umbrella, flew to Munich for a conference with Hitler that Mussolini had suggested. The Czechs were not invited. Nor was Czechoslovakia's other ally, the Soviet Union. British opinion was badly divided, but in the end Chamberlain gave Hitler the German-inhabited parts of Czechoslovakia, which in fact contained many Czechs and Jews. 'Munich' has since entered the world's vocabulary as code for shameful and cowardly behaviour, but Chamberlain for a time was wildly popular, and even the French prime minister, Édouard Daladier, was amazed when he discovered how popular he had become for giving up his country's ally. In the West and especially in a France that had lost almost half of the male wartime generation only twenty years before, where cripples hobbled around in any town or village demanding pensions that the country—given the failure of reparations—had no money to pay, no one wanted to fight again. Besides, there were widespread ideas that a war would be fatal, the destruction of civilization. Bombing aircraft, said many experts, would immediately smash London and Paris to pieces. The British expected 3,500 tons of bombs in London on the first day of war, with 600,000 killed in the first six months (in 1940–41, the figure was 60,000 casualties over seven months). Why fight to stop Germans in Czechoslovakia from joining Germany, if that was what they wanted to do? There was in London another calculation too. Rearmament had been going ahead, and it was quite efficiently done, with 'shadow' factories set up that would convert at once to war production when the time came. They were not quite ready. There was also a defence against the bomber, radar, because it alerted fast fighters to the danger, and they could fly up at once to oppose the bombers where previously they would have had to circle on patrols that ate up their fuel (a fighter could, at that time, stay up for only an hour and a half). A chain of radar stations was going up along the English coastline, but that too was not ready. Given that Germany's strength in bombing was considerably exaggerated, the attitudes of the men of Munich become understandable.

The outstanding opponent of appeasement was Winston Churchill, and his finest hour was approaching. He was born in the high summer of the Victorian empire, at Blenheim Palace, the historic seat of his eminent ancestor the Duke of Marlborough, who had famously defeated Louis XIV. Churchill was an

imperialist, and though Liberal to begin with, he became identified with reactionary causes. He lived British history, revelled
in the red colouring of the third of the globe that represented the
British Empire. Charm, wit, industry, and on occasion bullying
had carried him far, but he was also known for impulsive, con-
trarian behaviour; he opposed an obvious move towards Indian
independence, saying that she was 'no more a united nation than
the Equator'. He had argued that King Edward VIII should be
allowed to marry a twice-divorced American woman whom everyone detested, and he opposed the king's abdication. Churchill
was reactionary, and true reactionaries detested Adolf Hitler,
the most revolutionary figure in German history. He warned
again and again that conceding things to Hitler would only make
him worse. He had only a few supporters at the time of Munich,
though they were vociferous enough. But events bore him out.
On the night of 9 November 1938, which came to be known as
Kristallnacht, the Night of Broken Glass, and into the next
morning, there was a vicious outbreak of violence in Germany
and Austria against the Jews. Shops windows were smashed, the
streets were full of shattered glass, and synagogues were burned.
Ninety-one Jews were killed, and thousands more were herded
into camps and there made to pay a ransom for release; two-
thirds (some 120,000) of Vienna's Jews left, bringing terrible
tales to the many British families—including the Thatchers of
Grantham—who took them in. Obviously Munich had not 'ap-
peased' Hitler at all. He became more aggressive, making closer
links with Japan and Italy, to form a sort of Fascist bloc. He
had promised to leave the rest of Czechoslovakia alone, but

he did not. In March 1939, he broke up the country and marched into the Czech part. Slovakia, now independent, was a German puppet—in the war to come, a land flowing with milk and honey.

There was a wave of rage in London at Hitler's invasion of Czechoslovakia. Here was yet another German promise broken. March 1939 was the decisive moment as far as the British were concerned. They would never trust Hitler again. The British accelerated rearmament and started to look at other potential German victims, of which the first and most obvious was now Poland. One city on the Baltic coast was almost entirely German, Danzig (present-day Gdańsk). It lay at the mouth of the river Vistula, along which Poland's trade ran, and it had been quite rich through the Polish grain-trade. In 1919, the Poles meant to annex it, but Prime Minister Lloyd George shrank from any further humiliation of the Germans and he pushed for the city to be a Free State. The Poles then constructed an alternative port, and Danzig became an economic backwater. Once Hitler started to assert himself, the German population of Danzig responded, clamouring for union with Germany. In the spring of 1939 Hitler turned the heat up. Memel (present-day Klaipėda), a Lithuanian port, was German in much the same way and he sailed there to take it. Then he told the Poles he wanted Danzig. But here he had entered strange territory. Poland could quite easily have been a sort of large Slovakia, very Catholic and not very Slavonic: more anti-Russian than anything else. However, the country's past had sealed into it an immensely strong Catholic nationalism, and the government, which drew heavily on the military, was determined to stand up for itself, and not to have the fate of the Czechs. The British came along, and offered, after the destruction of Czechoslovakia, to 'guarantee' Poland's borders. The Polish foreign minister, Colonel Józef Beck, took a puff at his cigarette and said 'yes' to the British envoy's proposal. In the summer of 1939 Hitler went on and on about Danzig, but the British guarantee was an obvious obstacle. It was of course an ill-advised thing to have done and when they realized what they had done, the British themselves tried to escape. They gave the Poles almost nothing in the way of financial help, and then they wandered round cheapening the guarantee currency by guaranteeing anybody and everybody, including Greece, Turkey, and Rumania, the foreign minister of which had raised an alarm. All of this in retrospect looks mad. But Hitler had driven the world insane. That voice, its grievances, the enormous talent of the nation behind him: all well launched on a course of universal destruction, or so it seemed. Men alive in 1939 just said that as far as they were concerned, the war with Germany had already broken out that summer, and the pretext for it was neither here nor there. Hitler just had to be stopped.

Maybe Hitler would have paused over Poland, in view of the opposition that he had stirred up. But his intuition was again a sure guide, because, as so often happened with him, something did indeed turn up out of the crisis, and it stunned the world. The British and French, trying for some arrangement with Soviet Russia, had sent missions to Moscow. The Soviets discussed alliance but said their army would have to operate, if necessary, on

Polish territory. This, the Poles refused. The alliance discussions came to nothing, and then, all of a sudden, Stalin made a pact with Hitler, supposedly his deadly enemy. The German foreign secretary, Joachim von Ribbentrop, flew to Moscow on 22 August and signed it in the very early hours of the 24th. Here was another element in the inter-war story where pretensions were at a dangerous and corrupting remove from reality. In 1917 the Communists had seized power, had proclaimed the brotherhood of the working class, had won a civil war, and set about the transformation of peasant Russia. The Revolution offered in the event only tyranny and starvation, in millions, and it survived only through parasitical relations with the West. Of all people, the German industrialists kept it under way in the early Thirties, when there was a Five-Year Plan. Under its terms, grain was taken away from peasant children and from the seed-reserves of the farms, and fed to German pigs; eight million Ukrainians died, some as the result of cannibalism, and in return German machinery arrived in Russia. After Hitler came in, these economic relations declined, but then the Americans took over—100,000 of them, mainly engineers who were out of work. Then the Soviet Union went into the strangest paroxysm ever experienced by any country. Three-quarters of the senior officer corps, and then two-thirds of the Central Committee of the Communist Party were put on trial and murdered, an episode followed by weird massacres of innocents, their graves found much later. Yet here was the supposed champion of the world's industrial working classes, the arch-opponent of Adolf Hitler. No one could understand what was happening at the time, and historians have not done very well since. Most Western commentators at the time simply wrote off Stalin's state, and regarded Poland as, if anything, stronger ('that great virile nation', said Prime Minister Chamberlain). The Poles had after all preserved their independence in 1920 by defeating the Soviet ('Red') army, and this victory, combined with the purges, made the USSR's military value very unclear.

Hitler offered Stalin an agreement to partition Poland, and by extension other parts of Europe as well. Stalin, angered at being treated by the British like some sort of Emir of Bokhara, accepted. Poland would be split between Russia and Germany, and the Russians would also have a preponderant say elsewhere. There were economic arrangements—armaments for Stalin, raw materials for Hitler, which enabled Germany to avoid the troubles of blockade, and even to obtain rubber, oil, manganese, tungsten, and much else. Of course in a rational world there would not then have been a Second World War. If Russia and Germany were set on dividing Poland then there was nothing the French could do about it, still less the British, who did not have a large army and whose air force was only just coming up. But this was not a rational world: Hitler had maddened everyone. He sent his tanks over the Polish border on 1 September. The House of Commons revolted when the prime minister seemed to suggest that there might be mediation; and the French, fearing that the British would make an agreement with Hitler at their expense if they did not go along, joined in. When the British delivered their ultimatum, at around nine A.M. on 3 September, it contained an addition to the effect that the

French government would shortly be associating itself (as happened at five P.M.).

Hitler was at the desk in his study in the new Reich Chancellery—a room thirty yards by fifteen, with six large French windows overlooking the gardens, a huge map table made of rare Rosso Verona marble, and paintings of his heroes, Frederick the Great and Bismarck especially, glaring down from the walls. It was a room fit for a ruler of the world, and the Reich Chancellery had indeed been built by Albert Speer with just that in mind. Now, on 3 September, the British ambassador, in immaculate diplomatic uniform, called on the Foreign Ministry to present an ultimatum, in effect a declaration of war. Hitler's own foreign minister, von Ribbentrop, had assured him that this would not happen, and now he, standing by Hitler's desk, had to stand up to a glaring enquiry: Hitler sat silent for a minute or two and then said angrily, 'What now?' Ribbentrop had reckoned that England would never go to war for the particular cause that had come up, of all things, Danzig. But this was not a war about Danzig. Hitler had driven people into a corner, and they resisted. It was a war for honour—even then an old-fashioned concept, but one that still counted for much. Neville Chamberlain was not a man of humour and imagination, but he did see how it would all end. He spoke to the American ambassador, Joseph Kennedy (father of the future president), who noted Prime Minister Chamberlain's words in his diary: 'The futility of it all is the thing that is frightful; after all, [we] cannot save the Poles; [we] can merely carry on a war of revenge that will mean the destruction of all Europe.' He was soon to be replaced by a Winston

Churchill who, unlike Chamberlain, was a military product of the Victorian world, and who responded personally to the Nazi challenge. This was to be the first real rock that Hitler encountered. The rest—Versailles, League of Nations, Gold Standard, Little Entente—could be swept aside, but not Churchill.

WORLD WAR TWO

chapter two | GERMANY ASCENDANT

preceding page: German soldiers marching past the Arc de Triomphe, June 1940 (Bettmann/Corbis)

The war that broke out in 1939 had weird, symphonic under-
tones of historic European conflicts. Poland had once been a
great power, and bright Poles wondered why the country had
been overtaken, and in the end destroyed, by Germany and Russia. France had been her protector, and there had in the past
been wars about this—Napoleon's disastrous Moscow campaign
of 1812, and even, in a way, the Anglo-French attack on Russia
in the Crimean War of 1853–1856. These had effects beyond
Europe's confines, and so it was now: in December 1939 a German commerce raider, the *Graf Spee*, was chased into a South
American harbour and scuttled. But these first forty-one weeks
of World War Two constituted in essence the last European war,
a war very rapidly won by Germany. It had taken Napoleon five
years to become master of Europe, with the battle of Austerlitz
in 1805. It took Hitler nine months: his troops, in June 14,
1940, marched past the Arc de Triomphe that Napoleon had
put up in Paris to commemorate that battle. In the Foreign Office, in mid-September, Sir Alexander Cadogan said, 'We must

lose the war for four years before we win a decisive battle'—
curiously accurate.

Poland was the martyr of the Second World War, as Great
Britain was the hero, and the United States the victor. As with
many martyrs, Poland invited her fate. She might have opted to be
a German ally, in the expectation that she might gain something
in the western Ukraine, including Kiev, which had once been
ruled by Poland. Instead, her rulers firmly stayed with the British
and French, regarding them still as the victors of 1918. They,
like Poland, had profited from a highly artificial condition in
1918, when both Russia and Germany had been knocked out,
and the Poles thought of themselves as a great power, the eastern
bulwark of Europe. They had seen what had happened to the
Czechs, who had made concessions and then been broken at
Munich, and they would not be similarly budged, even when the
Nazi-Soviet pact was arranged. They refused each and every
small concession, in the expectation that British aircraft and
French tanks would make short work of the Germans. In September 1939 they did not last long. Hitler attacked without a
declaration of war, and much of their air force was destroyed
on the ground but most escaped to Rumania. Their armies were
placed well forward, for invasion of Germany, and were therefore cut off by German attacks from the Prussian north and the
Silesian west. They did make a brave stand near Warsaw, but
the city was savagely bombed, and then, on 17 September, the
Red Army came over the eastern borders. Seventy thousand men,
some ships, and some aircraft managed to escape, and a government in exile was set up in the west, but for the moment Poland

was occupied. Germany annexed much of the west, Soviet Russia the east. The remainder, called 'Government General', was under German occupation, and it was to be an occupation of immense murderousness, in which three million Polish Jews and three million non-Jewish Poles were killed. In the Soviet zone, there was mass deportation, and oppression was the fate of many Ukrainian nationalists as well, the supposed beneficiaries of Soviet rule.

The western Allies did nothing to help Poland, even though the Germans had to concentrate their resources there. France had spent seven billion francs on an enormous set of defences, the Maginot Line, built along its borders with Germany and Italy. Everyone expected it to keep France safe, but it firmly gave French strategy a defensive character. The French tiptoed from the Maginot, and when fired on, tiptoed back. London had expected a huge bombing campaign, and the air raid sirens went off after Chamberlain spoke on the BBC about the declaration of war. It was a false alarm: the Germans had no intention of starting a bombing campaign. There was some action at sea, but as the autumn started, nothing much happened in the west, and since tanks could not easily operate in mud, a few months of what came to be known as the 'phoney war' went on in a very hard winter. The western Allies did not want under any circumstances to attack—memories of the huge losses of twenty-five years before deterred them. The French had lost 1,500,000 men in the First World War, and the grim circumstances of the Thirties—Orwell said that Paris was a cross between a museum and a brothel—caused people just not to make babies. There had been a modest recovery in the summer of 1939, for the

150th anniversary of the Revolution, but its spirit no longer came through to the rat-trap faces of the politicians of the Republic's last phase. Besides, what help would come from the British? As in 1914, there would be a skirling of pipes at the gangplank in Boulogne, and a few Scottish regiments would arrive with the regimental mascot, a terrier, and a colonel smoking a pipe. The British after all could have stopped Germany in 1936, when Hitler re-occupied the Rhineland on France's borders. With British support, the French army, invoking various treaty clauses, could have invaded the Rhineland and enforced its demilitarisation. It had always been the British, the French felt, who prevented them from having proper security. The French Left had been seduced by Communism, and some of them denounced the war accordingly. The French Right had been shattered by the experience of a left-wing government in the years 1936–38, and much of it admired Nazism. This was not a formula for a happy alliance or a successful war effort. The cold winter of 1939–40 went ahead, with almost nothing to show for it on the Western Front except some digging. Belgium might have cooperated, but the country was badly divided, and Brussels did not want to provoke Hitler. The war shifted elsewhere, to the fringes.

The Nazi-Soviet Pact had included Baltic states in Stalin's sphere, and that meant Finland as well. The Finnish frontier, at Vyborg, was just a few miles from Leningrad, and Stalin, wanting security, demanded this and a naval base in southwestern Finland. The Finns, their country also an artificial victor of 1918, said no. But climate and terrain meant that they had a much more defensible arena than the Poles, and in late November, there came an extraordinary three-months' war, in the course of which the Red Army was humiliatingly defeated by ingenious Finns, on skis, emerging from the forests to trap whole divisions. The Finns had calculated that the British might come to the rescue, and indeed an expedition was assembled, but only for the reason that it would give the British an excuse to take a detour and block German deliveries, from Sweden, of iron ore. The French also produced a most extraordinary plan for their few transport planes to cross neutral Turkey at night and drop bombs on Baku, Azerbaijan, where there were oil wells—a plan sensibly vetoed by the British. But the Scandinavian expedition took time, Stalin moved in generals who had some idea of what they were doing, and mustered Russia's weight; the Finns gave way as their capital was bombed. The Anglo-French expedition to Scandinavia was forestalled, though the British meant to go on mining Norwegian waters. Before they could do so, Hitler infringed neutrality first: he secured the Scandinavian route, and on 9 April invaded Norway via Denmark.

The invasion of Norway was, strangely enough, one of the moments at which Hitler lost the war. The German navy, the *Kriegsmarine,* was never really large enough, but given the right circumstances it could have contributed decisively to an invasion of southern England. The Norwegians made this impossible. By freak shots, old Norwegian fortress guns and torpedoes in Oslo blew up the main German warship, and many destroyers were sunk in encounters with the British. This lucky break turned out to be decisive, in another way. It sank Chamberlain, and therefore removed any element in London that might have accepted some deal with Hitler. When the war broke out, Chamberlain had moved Churchill in as first lord of the admiralty—civilian head of the navy—in which office Churchill mismanaged the Norwegian affair. A battle occurred, for the first time directly, between German and British troops. The British did not do well; it was a very British start-of-a-war muddle. It also exposed a weakness— the overrating of sea power. There were monster battleships: the *King George V* cost as much as a modern factory and employed more men; she could carry 3,000 tons of fuel, as much as a tanker, and her engines generated as much horsepower as a power station. Her ten big guns weighed eighty tons each and fired a shell of 700 kg at a range of over twenty miles; her gun turrets weighed 1,500 tons. How could these monsters, which took two years to construct, ever be sunk? But, in fact, they were floating Maginots, and aircraft could demolish them.

Meanwhile, in London, Chamberlain was being blamed for everything that went wrong. There was a dramatic moment in the House of Commons, when in a vote against Chamberlain, the discontented imperialists, mostly Conservatives, combined with the Left against the PM, while other Conservatives abstained. One Conservative MP, Leo Amery (whose elder son, ironically, went on to broadcast on the Nazi radio and after the war would be hanged for treason) ended his denunciation of Chamberlain with Oliver Cromwell's famous words to a nuisance-parliament: 'You have sat too long here for any good you have been doing. Depart, I say, and let us have done with you. In the name of God, go!' This was a sign that a powerful new genie had emerged from the British bottle. The Establishment (as it came to be called) regarded Churchill as unstable, a maverick. Malcolm Muggeridge once remarked that, to succeed, British politicians have to be either a bookie or a vicar. In 1940, the bookie would be Lloyd George, while a possible replacement for Chamberlain was the very exalted, strangled-voice vicar-like Lord Halifax. The Establishment wanted him, but this was not the Establishment's hour, and besides, as Halifax himself said, he could hardly lead the country from the House of Lords. National opinion was expressed by the Labour Party, i.e., the trade unions, and Churchill formed a coalition government with it. He announced his policy: blood, toil, tears, and sweat, and that was indeed all that he could offer, as the vast battle now opened in the west. No Churchill emerged in France. As the classic author General Edward Spears said, 'The British middle classes were not scared, whereas the French bourgeoisie was gibbering with fright.'

Hitler had wanted to attack the previous autumn, 1939, but the German generals were not enthusiastic. They kept finding excuses—this unit not ready, the season too muddy, and so forth. Some of them talked even of overthrowing Hitler, though as ever these things never went beyond talk until much later. After prodding, the generals produced a scheme, a version of the original Schlieffen Plan of 1897, which had provided for the invasion of Holland and Belgium in the event of war with France. Then chance took a hand. An officer, given a lift in an aircraft from Cologne, took the plans along for a meeting. The aircraft missed its way, crash-landing in Belgium, and the papers, taken by the Belgians, though half-destroyed, were still readable. The Belgians passed them on to the French, and these confirmed what the

French High Command had thought would happen. There were two effects of this. The French were lured into one of the biggest military mistakes ever made, for the Germans changed their plan. Hitler had, as he often did, guessed at the truth, and that a plan of real boldness might succeed, whereas the generals vastly overrated the French army and were really thinking only of protecting the Ruhr industrial area from attack. A more ambitious general, Erich von Manstein, who understood what tanks and aircraft could do, had been suggesting a plan that was indeed very bold, and he had been sidelined by the High Command. By chance he met Hitler in Berlin and told him of the plan. There would be a feint in strength into Belgium and Holland, and that would draw the French in. But the real German attack would come through southeastern Belgium, a thickly wooded and hilly region called the Ardennes. It had few roads, not very good, but skilled traffic management could make them usable. A huge German force would come through the Ardennes and cross the frontier river Meuse at Sedan, where, seventy years before, the Prussians had defeated a French army and created a united Germany. Of course this movement could be stopped, in fact turned into catastrophe, if it went wrong, if, say, the tanks were attacked from the air and immobilized. Hitler took the chance.

On 10 May, the guns opened up on the Western Front, and here is one of the weirdest tales of military muddle and misunderstanding, ever. The French had made the tremendous mistake of investing a huge amount of effort in the protective fortress-system of the Maginot Line. André Maginot, a wartime sergeant,

had been war minister in 1929. French troops had been allowed
to occupy the Rhineland, for security purposes: no German invasion could happen. In 1929-1930, the British, in an effort to
'appease' Germany, took a lead in proposing the withdrawal of
Allied troops, and Maginot now said that security meant building elaborate fortifications. That program became a vast mill-
stone round the neck of the French. Obviously they would have
to keep a third of their forces stationed in it, for a defensive action. There was therefore no need for the Germans to station in
front of it more than some divisions of middle-aged veterans;
they could put their good troops and their armour elsewhere. In
that way the *Wehrmacht,* the unified armed forces of Germany,
though somewhat outnumbered in tanks, created a crushing local superiority where it mattered. They would move through Belgium, and that, the French expected. To keep the war away from
northern France the French therefore moved troops into Belgium, and, there, they encountered what they assumed, quite
wrongly, was the main German assault. This was Army Group
B, with thirty infantry and three Panzer armoured tank divisions
(each of some 200 tanks). They managed a real coup: they seized
the biggest fortress in the world, Belgian's Eben-Emael on the
Dutch border, by a brilliant tactic: glider-conveyed paratroops
landing on the roof in rubber shoes so as not to make a noise,
and dropping grenades through the ventilation shafts and gun
ports. Then, moving fast, they came up to the line of the River
Dyle, where they ran into the French army and almost all of the
British Expeditionary Force (BEF), which had moved into Belgium and was trying to reach Holland. This was the bulk of the

French army, and the best part. It was now pushed into an enormous elephant trap, leaving only thin and poor forces to defend France proper. The Germans had cracked the codes with which the French army communicated, knew what forces were kept in the Maginot Line, and could therefore guess where the French would have least strength. Given that the bulk of the French army, and all of the British Expeditionary Force, had been moved into Belgium, there were only weak forces between Belgium and the northern edge of the Maginot Line. These were strung out along the river Meuse, their leadership was dismal, and the men were the very picture of the demoralization of Third Republic France: dirty, sullen, cigarette-chewing, and smelling of cheap wine (of which the average Frenchman got through three litres every day, though in fairness it should be added that half of them were peasants, and the water was not reliable). Almost no one foresaw that the Germans could attack there, with enormous force, and indeed, in 1914, of the forty-seven German army trucks that had tried to use these roads, all but one had broken down. However, trucks and tanks had been considerably improved since those days and the Ardennes were now filled with long, long columns of nose-to-bumper tanks, vehicles, marching and cyling troops, with Luftwaffe cover. It was indeed a miracle of traffic management, and tanks that broke down were efficiently shunted to the side. The High Command had supposed that reaching the Meuse would take ten days, whereas the tank commander, Heinz Guderian, thought he could make it in four. As matters turned out, the Germans were on the Meuse within two days and at three P.M. on 15 May crossed it, with rubber dinghies.

The French were simply no match for the Germans. They were diverted and terrorized by Stukas, which dive-bombed almost vertically, their sirens emitting a howl, with a quarter-ton bomb, such that tanks and even artillery were paralyzed: in fact the Stukas were slow and vulnerable if gunners did not panic, but panic they did in 1940 because the Luftwaffe was managed with panache. A key German advantage now bore fruit in the Ardennes. The Luftwaffe had been constructed as an auxiliary to the army, as 'flying artillery', whereas the British RAF was designed for an independent air war, in which long-range bombing would take an important part (in 1936 this was formally recognized, in the setting up of Bomber Command). Now, the French and British bombers were alerted too late to the Germans' passage through the Ardennes, and when they did attack, in daylight, they were very easily dealt with by the Germans' Messerschmitt 109 fighters. Thirty-two 'Battle' bombers went into action on this first day, thirteen were destroyed, and the rest damaged. As the historian of the war Max Hastings says, these were 'coffins'. French pilots were demoralized with unreliable machines. The French fighters were extraordinarily slow and reluctant to respond; and the RAF was already worried as to how it could defend the British Isles if the fighters were involved in France. The Germans moved on. They got the tanks over the Meuse on 16 May and Guderian moved fast, ignoring orders to stop. This method has gone into history as 'Blitzkrieg', a translation of an Italian notion of 'lightning war', but that had not been the original idea of this campaign, which was to keep the Allies clear of Belgium, from where they could threaten the industrial Ruhr. It was Guderian's idea to sweep forward, and his superiors, including Hitler, worried that he would be attacked from the south, and cut off. But he went on, stopping to get gasoline from abandoned French garages, his men milking distressed and abandoned French cows. To his right, the dashing future Field Marshal Erwin Rommel also crossed the Meuse with tanks and guarded that flank. The open left flank might have been vulnerable, but here again the German infantry produced a miracle of speed, plodding through the brilliant early-summer weather for a week, managing forty miles each day, so that when eventually a French counterattack came, it failed against hardening resistance (and was slowed by the floods of refugees, trudging hopelessly along the roads). Rommel managed fifty miles in a day. Meanwhile Maurice Gamelin, the French commander, supposed that he would have to defend Paris, and so the commander of Guderian's Army Group A, Gerd von Rundstedt, was free to move towards the Channel, across flat country and with weather ideal for tanks. French tanks had not been grouped in such a way as to counter this—they were in the wrong place—and there was one surrender after another of French troops. Rundstedt reached Amiens and the old Somme battlefields, and then the Channel itself at Abbeville on 20 May, only a few days after the initial breakthrough on the Meuse. The French commander still worried that the Germans would head for Paris and was once again out-manoeuvred as they headed for the Channel. The disaster was that the British and French were now cut off in Belgium, and the Dutch had also collapsed: Rotterdam was heavily bombed. The French had done reasonably against Army Group

B in Belgium, and their performance much improved as they realized what was at stake, but now, cut off from France by Army Group A, they trudged with the British towards the sea, at the mercy of the Luftwaffe, and the Belgians in turn gave in. Later, the king of the Belgians was severely criticized, but the Belgian army did fight on long enough to enable the British and French to struggle towards the coast. By now the French, too, had been goaded, and the troops of Army Group B ran into resistance. A pocket of four divisions at Lille held the Germans up, and in admiration, they allowed the French an honourable surrender. The British and French managed a counter-attack near Arras on 21–22 May, and that caused some German alarm; besides, the Luftwaffe had been severely eroded: planes could not take the strain easily, and repair shops were over-burdened. Half of the bombers were out of action. On the 23rd, Hitler ordered a halt. The British commander, Lord Gort, was a good fighting soldier, and he resolved to save his own army from the Allied maelstrom, and withdrew in fighting order towards the Channel, at the port of Dunkirk. It was good defence-country with canals. The evacuation began on 27 May, and only ten thousand men were expected to get back. But British fighters now knocked out German bombers, the weather was at last favourable, and the destroyers that took off most of the soldiers were aided by some thousand other boats of all sorts. Some 340,000 men—229,000 British and the rest French and Belgian—were rescued, but they had left their heavy equipment behind.

Dunkirk was an extraordinary moment but came at the expense of the French, who had covered the retreat and now some

1,800,000 became prisoners of war. Both sides now recognized the extent of the German victory, and on 14 June Paris itself fell. The Maginot Line was captured intact, from the rear, and an armistice was signed on 22 June. German troops occupied northern and western France; the rest settled down under a collaborationist régime based in the spa town of Vichy, which busied itself with plans for national regeneration, with a hero of World War One, Marshal Philippe Pétain, aged eighty-four, heading it. It refused to hand over 400 captured Luftwaffe pilots to the British, and it did not scuttle the navy, to get it out of German clutches, as the British had energetically suggested. For a time, the French Empire went along, but even before the armistice, on 18 June, a dissident officer, Charles de Gaulle, went to London with a few sympathizers, where he established the 'Free French' and soon gained adherents in French Africa. Meanwhile France was to be ruthlessly exploited by the German occupants. In fear that the French navy might be commandeered by the Germans as well, the British sank much of it at harbour in Algeria, while French naval commanders elsewhere made terms with the British. During this desperate time, Mussolini at last entered the war.

Great Britain was now without continental allies, and with the Italian intervention, even the Mediterranean was no longer open. At the time of Dunkirk, an element in the Cabinet had wavered, wondered about peace, and, briefly, Churchill considered it. There had been a comparable situation in 1917, when the Germans were dictating terms to defeated Russia and had hinted to the British that a deal might be done between them at France's expense. Prime Minister Lloyd George had given this some thought and waved it aside: a Germany controlling Russia would be unbearable and unbeatable. In 1940 this was still more obviously true, and Churchill stuck his chin out: we fight on. It was an extraordinary decision, but he had national backing, and members of the Cabinet, some weeping in exultation, cheered him. Hitler himself could not quite understand it, and offered peace terms, though in a triumphalist tone that begged for the answer 'no'. Churchill stated his war aims. These were simple enough: Germany should give up her gains and give a clear guarantee by deeds that she would not repeat her crimes.

Modern war develops its own momentum, and reasoning is left behind. As far as most of the British public were concerned, the war had already broken out in the summer of 1939, and they were not going to give up now. But there seemed to be very little hope. The German war machine gathered on the other side of the Channel, and its leaders drew up plans for the invasion of the British Isles, *Unternehmen Seelöwe*—Operation Sea Lion. But the Germans had (in part because of the Norwegian campaign) far too few warships to ensure success, and the Luftwaffe had to provide cover for the barges that were assembled on the French coast. The Luftwaffe's goal was to knock the RAF out of the sky. Eventually, bombers would come over, with fighter protection, and terrorize the British into surrender. The German plan had not been thought through, and there were not enough fighters; from 10 May to 31 July, the Luftwaffe lost almost 4,400 planes. The RAF, operating near base, could be far freer with fuel, whereas the Luftwaffe men had to go back to base. *Unternehmen Adlerangriff* (Operation Eagle Attack), the German code name for the campaign, began officially on 13 August, and the Battle of Britain, as it came to be called, lasted from 15 August to 15 September. To begin with, the Germans' objective was not clearly laid out and they lost heavily—on 15 August, seventy-five aircraft to thirty-four. The chief of the RAF Fighter Command, Hugh Dowding, held his men back from the sort of dogfights in the sky that made for good propaganda, and used them instead to destroy the bombers. Then the Luftwaffe switched targets, trying to smash the airfields in southern England; this time round it was the British who suffered higher losses. Then an accident happened. A German flier needed to lighten his load to fly home, and on August 24 dropped his bombs over what he thought was countryside. It was blacked-out London. The RAF thought that bombing of cities had begun, and responded, with an attack on Berlin. Hitler lost patience and ordered the bombing of London, civilians and all. On 7 September London became the target, for a week, until 15 September, when the Germans made a final big effort. This time the British lost twenty-six planes, the Germans sixty (the British gave out that the true number was 185). The Luftwaffe altogether lost 1,773 planes and the British 915, and there was another figure, not much noticed at the time: British output of fighters was higher than German. They had rearmed later, and had thought things through, whereas the Germans for once suffered from having been first off the mark, had many competing agencies, and even seventeen different research laboratories. When Lord Beaverbrook took charge of aircraft production, he ended the nonsense by which there were three civil servants for every aircraft. He cut corners, was rude over the telephone, ignored committees. As Alistair Horne said, it was 'rule by roar'. Aircraft production was a considerable British success story, whereas the Luftwaffe's affairs were a mess, ending aptly at Munich in 1945, when the first jet fighter had to be towed onto the field by oxen, to save fuel. The British produced 500 planes per week in 1940, the Germans half as many.

The invasion of Britain was now cancelled. For retaliation, Hitler and Goering ordered the continued bombing of London and for the next six months, that went ahead, weather permitting. It was a national epic, symbolized for the world by the photograph of St Paul's Cathedral surrounded by the flames from the burning buildings all around. Nine thousand tons of high explosives were dropped every month until March 1941. The dockyards of the East End were a particular target, and the Cockney population there spent its nights in shelters and sometimes deep down in the London Underground, where discipline was remarkable, as George Orwell noted, and outbreaks of panic were few. He also noted the extraordinary solidarity that prevailed, and wrote a somewhat sentimental account of it (*The Lion and the Unicorn*), as a sort of socialist emancipation. Other people were emancipated differently. Graham Greene had left his family behind at Beaumont Street, Oxford, and was having an affair in a flat near the British Museum. He was the building's fire watchman, was caught by a bomb, and had to claw his way from the upper floor of the house that he had been inspecting. The experience caused him to abandon the girl (she was apparently rather ugly) and it enters literature, and film, as *The End of the Affair.* There were many such emancipations in the Second World War.

Over all of this stood now the giant figure of Churchill, who had found his moment. With very little dissension, he led a nation united in defiance in what he called 'Our Finest Hour'. But the real hope could only be that the United States would intervene, and this was not an easy matter. An American law enforced strict neutrality. There had been a huge reaction against the First World War. Many Americans felt that they had somehow been tricked into it, for the sake of East Coast financial interests, and President Franklin Roosevelt's hands were tied. In theory, arms could not be sold except for cash down, not credits. The British had invested hugely in the United States, and had enormous assets there. These were now compulsorily sold off almost at fire-sale prices in order to pay for armaments. However, there were German U-boats in the Atlantic, and American trade was menaced; and in any case Roosevelt knew very well that if the British collapsed, then the United States would face a German-Russian world, with a Japan already expanding not just in China but elsewhere in east Asia, where there were considerable American interests. The two Atlantic Powers therefore cooperated in ways not forbidden by formal law. Roosevelt gave fifty American destroyers to the British to defend their shipping, in exchange for a lease on bases in the British West Indies. Meanwhile, American warships were authorized to fire on German U-boats and by October 1940 were doing so. Hitler gave strict orders that there was to be no retaliation, since the two countries were not at war, but on occasion his captains were provoked and in one case there was retaliation. From Hitler's point of view in a sense he was already at war with the United States. The essential battle was in fact that of the Atlantic, as more and more German U-boats now came into production and threatened the British lifeline.

Meanwhile, the British had considerable strength in a crucial area, their native genius for gathering intelligence, played as a sort of game. They had for the most part cracked the secret German codes and in effect replicated the Germans' Enigma encoding machine, fabulously complicated. Previously, British Intelligence had used the term 'most secret' for the most essential secrets crucial to national security. Now, for the breaking of German (and other) codes, there was a new higher level: 'ultra secret', or Ultra. (Enigma and Ultra mark vital stages in the development of the computer.) Of course if the Germans knew that the British were decoding their secrets, then the game would have been over. So, on occasion, to conceal from the Germans that their plans were known, British commanders deliberately avoided taking actions that would have saved them from defeat: the most obvious case being the failure to defend the main airport on Crete in May 1941 when the Germans were about to attack. By 1943 Hitler had become so convinced that someone close to him was revealing military secrets that he had lunch alone, at most with his valet, Straub.

All in all, by the early months of 1941, Hitler was in a frustrated mood. He could tell that the Americans were arming, that they might well intervene. He had an idea that he himself would not live to a ripe old age, and he said often enough that if it were not for him, Germany would never have got to where she was. Opinion at home was waiting for the next miracle, and the people meanwhile were having to put up with tiresome privations that did not make sense in the war as it then was. In these circumstances, Hitler thought to himself: the only real hope for the British was that the Russians were still well and truly present. He would knock them out.

chapter three | BARBAROSSA

preceding page: Citizens of Lwów cheering the arrival of German troops, July 1941 (Berliner Verlag/Archiv/dpa/Corbis)

When France fell, Hitler was overwhelmed in the euphoria of it all. He went back to Germany through Strasbourg, capital of an Alsace that once more was German, and there he was cheered to the skies. The Germans had been spared the long war that they had expected, and their casualties had been extraordinarily low—under 30,000 killed. There was now no continental enemy left. In 1918, which had been Hitler's geopolitical starting point, Russia had collapsed, and with the Treaty of Brest-Litovsk, in March, between the Russians and the Germans, the German generals laid down terms for the setting up of an eastern European empire of which Berlin would be the capital. Hitler had begun to rebuild the capital on these lines, and in the concentration camps, which were usually near stone quarries, slaves laboured to produce the building material for the giant constructions to come. The Reich Chancellery had already been built, complete with be-swastika'd eagle clutching the globe, and there was to be a monster boulevard, the 'east-west axis', allowing the vastly powerful to travel by fast motorcade through jubilant crowds.

In nine months, Hitler had achieved more than any German ruler before him. Now he could go back to the original programme of *Mein Kampf,* as inspired by Brest-Litovsk: a vast Europe ruled by Adolf Hitler. The time had come to move against Soviet Russia.

But to invade Russia, Hitler needed the British to come to terms with him, and they did not. Instead they brushed aside his peace offer, in July. Then they fought back, and Hitler's concentration was diverted to the south and west, away from Russia. He had to cooperate with her, and Stalin was only too willing. He had after all faced down what he regarded as a vast military conspiracy to overthrow him, and had demoted, imprisoned, or killed off 35,000 senior officers, including three of the nation's five marshals and some of the best military inventors; the survivors were not up to a German *Blitzkrieg* and he therefore tried to buy Hitler off. Two million tons of oil, 140,000 of manganese, 26,000 of chromium, and much else passed the frontier, in return for military exports that were not faithfully delivered. There was much surrealism as the diplomatic niceties were observed: Sergei Eisenstein, the brilliant maker of the anti-German historical epic film of 1938 *Alexander Nevsky,* was put in charge of a production of Richard Wagner's *Die Walküre* at the Bolshoi Theatre, and relations in occupied Poland were quite cordial, while Gestapo officers compared security notes and held competitive skiing events with their counterparts in the NKVD, Stalin's secret police. For Hitler's fifty-first birthday, Stalin made him a present of fifty German Communists, one of whom, Margarete Buber-Neumann, wrote a book of memoirs of her times in the camps (she said that in the Soviet ones there were occasional touches of humanity: in the German ones, more efficient, none). There were clashes of interest, of course, but war was not a likely outcome. Hitler had other things to do.

Churchill and Hitler looked for ways to fight each other. In the six months following the Battle of Britain, the Blitz on British towns went ahead, and did much damage—3,500,000 dwellings were by May 1941 damaged or destroyed, along with the House of Commons and much of the City of London, and 30,000 people were killed. Neither production nor morale was dented. On the other hand, the British themselves, though enthusiastic about bombing the enemy, did not have the technical requirements, and lost a bomber for every ten tons of bombs dropped—a rate of loss that could not be sustained and that did little damage in any event. There was a more dangerous situation still at sea, where German U-boats could use French ports and thereby be far closer to the killing grounds in the Atlantic. In April 1941 nearly 700,000 tons of shipping went down, more than could be replaced. But the Germans had too few submarines, and in any case the British knew where they were, because they had cracked the German codes. When in 1940–41 Allied ships began systematically sailing in convoys, the sinkings declined dramatically (as had also happened in 1917). And the United States gave important help, protecting the sea lanes beyond Iceland. For a time Hitler considered attacking the British position in the Mediterranean, and he approached Spain's Franco to see what he thought. Franco was proud, would not be treated as if Spain was one of Hitler's satellite states. In any case, Spain was a wreck, after the Civil War, and Franco was still vindictively fighting it.

He got the Gestapo to extradite from Paris exile the aged Luis Companys, former president of Catalonia—who had in fact saved Franco's brother from being shot in 1936—and had him shot. The British ambassador had been sent £10,000,000 to bribe Spanish generals if it seemed they might be entering the war, but Spain kept out: Franco was cautious, and in any case Hitler did not want to have to arbitrate over the claims of France, Italy, and Spain. Seeking support, Nazi agents went round the Middle East, but got nowhere: expressions of sympathy, yes (including from a young officer, Gamal Abdel Nasser) but no effective contribution. But this casting-about nonetheless developed into something different.

The European war turned into a world war, oddly enough, because of the Italian connection. In the summer of 1940, there was some question of the Mediterranean's becoming *mare nostro*—our sea. The Italians had long resented French predominance in North Africa, and now they were in a position to evict the British, they thought, from Egypt. With the British and French defeat, they could set up a Balkan empire at the expense of Greece; they had already seized Albania and the Aegean islands. Mussolini said to his foreign minister, Galeazzo Ciano, who was also his son-in-law, that it was time to match the Hitler who had once been his pupil. In October, into Greece Mussolini charged. It ended in disaster. The Greeks knew how to fight in Balkan mountains, the Italians, not; they froze and starved. The Italians had another disaster when they attempted to invade Egypt. It was maybe a sign that Churchill did not really fear a German invasion of England, because he sent there the remaining tanks.

Over 200,000 Italian soldiers moved east in September and were attacked by a brilliant British general, General Richard O'Connor, who understood how to use tanks (he outflanked the Italians in the desert and attacked them from the west, as the Italians were busy dealing with their major enemy, their own sanitation, resulting in dysentery and worse). Then another brilliant British commander, Admiral Andrew Cunningham, showed what aircraft could do against ships, and sank half of the Italian capital ships, the most important vessels, at Taranto in November. So far, so good. But Hitler was drawn into both Balkan and Egyptian theatres. He did not have much interest in Egypt, but sent his most enterprising general, Erwin Rommel, with two Panzer divisions; Rommel attacked when the British were particularly weak. O'Connor had been captured in a freak incident, and the other officers were not of his calibre. To make matters worse for the British, they decided to assist Greece. They were spreading themselves too thin. Hitler had at first said he did not want to hear about Greece, 'this southeastern mission'. It was thrust upon him, first of all because he was very dependent upon the oil of Rumania and in October 1940 had sent a military mission to protect it against a possible Russian or British incursion. Then in April he moved into Yugoslavia, using Bulgaria as an ally; and from there, he invaded Greece. The British suspended their North African campaign to assist Greece, and calamity ensued. The RAF had been kept mainly at home, and the Luftwaffe deployed 1,500 bombers in the Mediterranean. Onto Crete, in May, the German paratroops descended, and 13,000 British troops were captured.

The Mediterranean formed the backdrop to Hitler's most ambitious campaign—the attack on Russia. Once he had given up serious consideration of North Africa, he was free to revert to his original scheme. At the turn of 1940–41, various quarrels came up with the Russians, which in any event needed clarification. Berlin had made an arrangement with the Japanese in September 1940, which encouraged them to take over land in the Far East, as the European empires there collapsed. But the Japanese had their own quarrels with Moscow, over border territories in northeastern China. To sort things out on a global scale, Hitler asked Vyacheslav Molotov, in charge of Soviet foreign affairs, to come to Berlin in November 1940. He extended the kind of project that Napoleon had offered Tsar Alexander: in alliance with Italy (for Africa), Germany (for Europe), and Japan (for East Asia), the USSR could have Iran and India. But Molotov wanted the Straits from the Black Sea to the Mediterranean, Turkish territorial waters, and was not to be fobbed off. He complained about German interference in Finland and Rumania, about which Stalin was hypersensitive, as they were close and hostile neighbours (Rumania had had a Fascist coup). A British bombing raid occurred while these discussions went on (Churchill joked that it was his revenge for not being invited) and, as Hitler had been claiming the war was really over, Molotov said, 'If the war is over, why are we sitting in this shelter?' He showed no interest in Hitler's schemes, but concentrated on Turkey. Molotov was one of the most irritating negotiators ever: his main word was 'no'. Perhaps, had he given in to Hitler's blandishments, and accepted Iran instead of Turkey, matters would have developed differently. At any rate, when he left, Hitler ordered preparation of a huge attack on Soviet Russia, with the code name Barbarossa which referred to a crusading emperor in the Middle Ages.

Hitler could see that time was not working for him. On the contrary, the Americans were mobilizing a formidable economy and already were engaged in the North Atlantic against German submarines. The best short-term response was to strengthen the alliance with Japan. Since the world slump of 1929, Japan, in the grip of a militaristic semi-dictatorship, was desperate for raw materials and markets. From 1931 onward, she had occupied the Chinese seaboard, and there were tensions with the Americans, who had a sort of protectorate over China. The anti-Comintern Pact had never developed into a proper alliance. But when Hitler conquered Europe, he had of course a great deal to offer, as far as the Dutch and French possessions in East Asia were concerned. The Japanese needed oil, and could get it from the Dutch East Indies. Accordingly in September 1940 they signed a Tripartite Pact with Italy and Germany, and each signatory pledged to declare war if another were attacked. Hitler did not want Japanese help against Russia, but did expect his new ally to keep the United States busy. The Japanese then followed his logic, and concluded a non-aggression pact with Moscow—after which they bombed China mercilessly and prepared an invasion of Southeast Asia.

The Japanese-Soviet pact was a weird way to prepare for the Germans' war with Russia, in which a Japanese invasion of Siberia might have been decisive. But it was not the only weird aspect of Barbarossa. After it had all gone wrong, there was a wrangle as to who was responsible. But almost none of the generals objected as Barbarossa was planned and initiated, whereas they had done so before the attack on France. Because their Führer had defeated France, they had swallowed Hitler's own myth, and they had swallowed another one as well, that of Soviet weakness. In this they were in good company, for almost the whole of informed opinion agreed: the Germans would win in ten days (British Intelligence), a month (Stafford Cripps, British ambassador), 'a possible maximum of three' (the American military). Stalin probably thought, 'a weekend'. He had feared some sort of military coup against him and destroyed the senior ranks of the Red Army, the men who had thought through strategy and understood military engineering. Men such as the future Marshal Konstantin Rokossovsky were having their teeth knocked out and toes broken until Barbarossa rescued them. The overall impression in the western world was that Russia was collapsing. The place had supposedly rationalized peasant agriculture, but famine had resulted—Russians did not eat at pre-revolutionary standards until 1952, if then. Hitler is said to have remarked, We'll kick the door in and the house will fall down.

The strategic planning for Barbarossa was slapdash, and almost no one objected. Hitler was a provincial figure, and had shot far beyond his natural level; success like this turned his head. A Bismarck or a Churchill could control success of this order, a Hitler not. He thought he was infallible, that 'Providence' was looking after him. He was going to be Germany's Alexander the Great, overthrowing the tyrannical empire of the East, and large numbers of western Europeans, as with the Greek city-states in Alexander's time, volunteered to join in: a Spanish division would fight outside Leningrad, there were Italian, Hungarian, and Rumanian armies, and Dutch, French, Scandinavian SS legions. However, the great danger in attacking Russia was that the invaders would get swallowed up, and lose the place because the country, in the provinces always backward, had become under Communism impossibly so. Europe had roads, villages, churches, peasant customs, small provincial towns. By contrast, Russia was just, as Victor Hugo had said about Napoleon's retreat from Moscow, 'after one white plain, another white plain'. But Hitler, without dissent from the generals, told them to aim for a north-south line, roughly from Archangelsk to the Crimea. Again, because of the western victory and the naval war, economic preparation had been poor, the level of civilian life in Germany was not seriously cut back, whereas the divisions became somewhat weaker: the forces against the USSR counted hardly more tanks and aircraft than in the French campaign. A Panzer division was supposed to have 17,000 men and around 200 tanks, with motorized infantry, but the number of tanks was reduced to 125. German tanks were generally inferior to the Russians' T-34 medium and KV heavy tanks, as the guns had less range and the armour was not as thick. Hitler had made no provision for winter clothing, or for elementary items such as antifreeze. The three million Germans and 3,400 tanks (with 3,000 aircraft) were moved up to the Polish and Rumanian borders efficiently enough, and if Soviet observers wondered what was going on, they were fobbed off with an absurd excuse: training exercises.

Notoriously, Stalin had warning after warning of the impending invasion. His own spy in Tokyo knew; Churchill knew, from the de-coding of German documents; deserters from the German armed forces knew; and there was even an ingenious dummy Communist spy-ring set up by the British, 'Lucy', in Switzerland, which passed on the truths that the British were learning. Stalin would not have taken information from the British at face value—he did not even bother to have the endless reports of the famous 'Cambridge Five' spies translated—but he might believe in Lucy, thought the cunning British. To no avail. In his life, there was only one man Stalin trusted, wrote Aleksandr Solzhenitsyn. Stalin distrusted Lev Trotsky, he distrusted the Politburo, he distrusted the generals, he distrusted the writers. The only man Joseph Stalin trusted was Adolf Hitler. The last train bearing the goods with which Stalin proposed to placate Hitler trundled with a whistle on the railway bridge over the River Bug at Brest-Litovsk at two A.M. on 22 June 1941. The attack came at three A.M. A Communist deserter, a German soldier with a Communist background, swam the river and warned the Russians what was coming. He was shot. Some writers have argued that, from the layout of Soviet troops on the border, Stalin was planning to attack first. In fact, Hitler used Russian troop movements there as an excuse to invade. But the Soviets' earlier frontier fortifications had been neglected as their border in 1939 moved a hundred miles forward into Poland. New ones were badly constructed, but troops were moved in anyway. But that action reflected something else—that Stalin rated his own forces' loyalty and competence so low that he would trust them only in the foremost front line, and in great unwieldy formations, with a cordon of NKVD troops behind ready to shoot any men who fled in panic. That in the longer term Stalin needed to prepare for war with Hitler was obvious, that revolutionary military doctrine would call for flag-waving offensives was clear. But Stalin abased himself not to be attacked there and then. When the attack came, Molotov asked the German ambassador, Werner von der Schulenburg: 'What have we done to deserve this?' The answer was: exist. Hitler expected to shut down the entire Soviet show, and gave orders for all Communists and Jews, whom he held responsible for Communism, to be executed on sight. Nazism represented the triumph of European civilization, and the barbarian Russians, manipulated by evil-minded Jews, needed to be eliminated.

Between three and four A.M. on 22 June 1941, the German army moved forward. The main force was Army Group Centre, commanded by a general, Fedor von Bock, who was very tall and came from a Prussian military dynasty that included a chief of the General Staff in World War One, Erich von Falkenhayn. Bock intimidated even Hitler, for a time, and so got his way, which became, for other generals, increasingly difficult. Army Group Centre, with half of the forces, was to head for Moscow, across mostly flat terrain, and on the way, some four hundred miles ahead, there was something of an obstacle—the narrow neck of land between the rivers Dniepr and Dvina, flowing a long way to, respectively, the Black Sea and the Baltic. This was a traditional invasion route, and there was an old fortress on it, at Smolensk. It was to see very serious fighting when the time came. But to start with, the Germans had an enormous triumph. The Red Army was superior in numbers of tanks and aircraft, though much of the equipment was obsolete. Only platoon commanders' tanks had radios, whereas all German tanks had them. The very first result of the Germans' tactical surprise was that over 1,000 Soviet planes were destroyed on the ground as the sun came up and the Germans flew undetectably out of it. The pilots had had only four hours' flight training and feared that, if there was an accident, they would be charged with sabotage, so did not volunteer for more. There were large mechanised corps, but they were too large for the command system, with a thousand tanks each and 36,000 men, quite incapable of German nimbleness. In the first week, most of the mechanised corps were also destroyed.

The Germans' progress was spectacular—the more so as in many places, such as the southeastern Polish city of Lwów (now Lviv), they were ecstatically received by Ukrainians there as liberators. The tactical preparation and intelligence were very thorough, and there was immediate confusion on the Soviet side, made all the worse because of the orders from headquarters to counter-attack, with bewildered divisions being mown down. The general who had commanded the key Western Army Group, Dmitry Pavlov, was relieved of his command, tried for criminal incompetence and treason, and shot. On the left of Bock's group, Hermann Hoth's Panzer Group reached Vilna, on the way to Minsk, and split and broke through two Soviet army groups by

25 June. On the southern flank, Guderian moved forward to create a huge pocket of four Soviet armies. The pincers drove to the Berezina River and closed, infantry following to seal the pocket. In the north, by 26 June, the Germans had bridgeheads across the Dvina River, and in the centre Panzer movements around Minsk trapped Russians in huge pockets, at Białystok and elsewhere: cut off from supplies, not knowing what was going on, and bombed to pieces by the Luftwaffe. By 29 June, 290,000 had surrendered, though the fortress of Brest-Litovsk held out until 12 July. The Russians there in under three weeks lost half a million men, 1,200 aircraft, 5,000 tanks, and 10,000 guns. There was a similar triumph with the Northern Army Group, which took Lithuania in two days, one corps sending its fast group to cover fifty miles on the first day to prepare a vital river crossing. The Southern Army Group was slower, as it faced the strongest Soviet force. That was to count in the Germans' favour as things turned out. Gerd von Rundstedt, running Ewald von Kleist's 1st Panzer Group as in the Dunkirk days, came within a few miles of Kiev by 11 July but could not take the place. This failure invited another piece of catastrophism from Stalin when the time came. Stalin himself was prostrate for several days, and only broadcast on 3 July, by which time a central defence authority had been established after the Politburo had very gingerly dared to offer advice (when the men arrived at his suburban residence, Stalin thought that they had come to depose him). There was a remarkable mass mobilization, as civilians up to the age of sixty were set at least to digging defences, sometimes twelve hours every day and under fire, and most quite pointless.

There was one Russian both bright enough to understand what was happening and tough enough to keep his nerve—Marshal Georgy Zhukov, Stalin's trouble-shooter. Somehow, and very rare this was, he had a manner such that Stalin could not browbeat him as he did the others around him, and he had also won a remarkable battle in 1939 that had grown out of frontier skirmishes against the Japanese. He knew what he was doing, and ruthlessly put it through. The existing front-line troops on the Russians' Western Army Group should just be sacrificed on a line along the defensible rivers as they ran north-south, the Dvina and the Dniepr, before it reaches Kiev. There was the neck of land around Smolensk, a position whose flanks were relatively secure. A stand would be made here, after which reserves would have to be built up behind them and brought in especially from Siberia. There were in fact 600 Soviet divisions with at least some military training—14,000,000 men (including Central Asians), twice what the Germans expected. Besides, with an extraordinary piece of improvisation, a good part of industry was evacuated to the Urals: N. A. Voznesensky of the Five-Year Plan office had ordered this on 24 June, and the order affected the industries of the Ukrainian Donets basin and the lower Dniepr at Zaporozhye, where the turbines had been destroyed. Five hundred enterprises and 500,000 workers were taken out of the Moscow region, enabling the arms industry, with 10,000-ton hydraulic presses, to survive in the Urals and beyond, in Kazakhstan. Once there, the factory bosses had to rationalize and make proper use of their machinery (as also happened with aircraft production in England). Something of a miracle followed.

Zhukov's calculation was successful at least in so far as there was another disaster that held the Germans up. The pocket at Minsk resisted, but in the end collapsed, and by mid-July the Germans were into the Smolensk land bridge, the last geographical obstacle before Moscow. They were also well on the way to Leningrad. Then the big German decision had to be taken. Were they to make for Moscow as Bock leading the centre group wanted, or should they head instead for the raw material areas of the Ukraine? The latter would mean shifting Guderian's Panzer group towards the south. These debates occurred in the context of a hardening of the Soviet lines. There was a fight for the land bridge between these, at Smolensk, in which a Russian counter-attack at Yelnya, on the Dniepr south of Smolensk, worked out quite well—the first serious German setback. The Russians stood their ground, despite encirclement, for two months, forcing the Germans to stay and fight. The German armed forces, the *Wehrmacht,* had lost 213,000 men, and Bock in any case had to stop because the maximum range of their mobile infrastructure was 400 miles—Smolensk, as it happened. Tanks and trucks needed rest and repair, whereas in France that distance meant the Channel, along pleasant roads. The same pause came in the Baltic states, although there the population, liberated from Stalin, were helpful.

The door had been kicked in and the house was indeed falling down, but only in places. It was, after all, a vast house, the Soviet Union, sixty times the size of Germany. A month's halt was called, while the army re-stocked in everything. Now there was a row, the first of several bitter ones, between Hitler and the generals.

They said: Moscow. Hitler said that Moscow did not matter, that this was a war for coal and oil, that he wanted southern Russia. Hitler ordered a swing to the south, to trap the Soviet armies around Kiev, and he was very lucky, in that Stalin refused to let them withdraw. Guderian's Panzer Group moved south, Kleist's Panzer Group moved north from Kremenchug, and in a pocket around Gomel, two vast Russian armies were destroyed, with a loss of 500,000 troops by 17 September, the greatest single German victory. This opened the way to the Donets basin, the Crimea, and even the Caucasus. Kiev fell, with 665,000 prisoners, civilian and military. The Luftwaffe had cooperated brilliantly with the Panzers over the dry ground, and the Russians could not adapt. In the south, the Germans rolled forward after Kiev: Kleist crossed the Dniepr, making for Rostov-on-Don, and cut off 100,000 Russians at Berdyansk on the Sea of Azov (6 October). Kharkov fell on 24 October, Rostov on 20 November, and the Crimea was overrun save for the fortress port of Sevastopol and the small peninsula stretching towards the northern Caucasus, Kerch. In the north, the Germans were bombarding Leningrad in mid-September, the start of that city's martyrdom. The Finns were also now taking their revenge by besieging the city from the northwest, the Karelian Isthmus and Vyborg. By 15 September Leningrad was cut off, and the Germans decided just to let it starve. A million deaths were to follow, more than for the entire British and American war efforts combined. In that winter the city kept going because of a *voie sacrée,* a thin lifeline over Lake Ladoga, near the city, and survived because in January both evacuation and supply grew, as the ice thickened. It also mattered that the Finns knew when to stop. They took back what had been theirs in 1939, but their leader, Marshal Carl Gustaf Emil Mannerheim, knew his Russians, having been a Tsarist cavalry general, and said, If we do more than this, they will never forgive us. Leningrad survived to an important extent because of the Finns, *chukhontsy*, as the Russians mockingly call them (it refers to their famed drinking habits).

In early October 1941 came the great German assault on Moscow—Operation Typhoon. Guderian's Panzer group moved up through Oryol, Bryansk, and Tula, now famous names in the military history of Russia. From the north came the Panzer group of another warrior, Hoth, via Vyazma and the Napoleonic battlefield of Borodino. The Germans had nearly a million men, 1,700 tanks, and 14,000 guns though only 550 planes (the Luftwaffe had lost 1,603 aircraft and 1,028 had been damaged). The plan was for the usual pincers—focused on Vyazma and Bryansk, and after that, from north and south, on Moscow. The Red Army had 1,250,000 men, 1,000 tanks, and 7,600 guns, with under 1,000 aircraft, but there were still problems as regards training and quality. The two Panzer groups got through the uncompleted defences on the northern side, and when they met at Vyazma they encountered a huge pocket. It went on fighting, as the French had failed to do in similar circumstances a year before, and kept thirty German divisions occupied; many escaped to set up lines at Mozhaisk, west of the capital. At Bryansk to the south there was a similar story—Guderian enveloped the Red Army via Oryol and took Bryansk on 6 October, with much help from the air. Two Soviet armies were encircled but did not surrender, and a new line was set up around Mtsensk. By 7 October 1941, the German offensive ran into the problem of the Russian autumn and the mud that came with it. Everything stuck fast. Now, new Russian T-34 tanks could ambush the German tanks from woods, and they savaged the inferior Panzer IVs, which with short 75-mm guns could only destroy a T-34 from behind. In mid-October, at the Mozhaisk line, the Germans ran into serious defences. Zhukov now came from Leningrad to take charge of the defence of a Moscow in uproar.

This was the famous Moscow panic, which entered the subconscious of everyone who lived through it. The Communist Party, the General Staff, the government left in special trains for Samara, on the Volga; there was looting, and in the new apartment buildings of the centre, management connived with looters until the NKVD moved in to shoot. Stalin publicly stayed in the city so that he could preside over a great parade for the thirty-fourth anniversary of the Revolution on 7 November. By 13 October the Germans reached a line stretching from Kalinin (called Tver when Modest Musorgsky drank himself to death there) to the towns of Volokolamsk, eighty miles northwest of Moscow, and Kaluga, ninety miles southwest of the capital. Moscow itself was transformed into a fortress as women and boys shovelled tons of earth, without machinery to help; and the city was now attacked from the air. The Germans tried to bypass these defences and did well, as the ground hardened, though the industrial city of Tula held, 120 miles to the south of Moscow, and on 18 October they attacked the Mozhaisk lines, taking Voloko-

Iamsk on 27 October. But the weather now told, as it became an adventure to make a motor work, so that the supply problems were formidable: the lack of winter clothing really mattered as the temperature dropped and frostbite increased. Only a third of their motor vehicles were still functioning, and infantry divisions were at one-third strength. Six hundred thousand strong German horses were weakened or collapsed and died.

By 15 November 1941, when the ground froze, the final test began. Two German Panzer groups were set to encircle the capital from the north, and a Panzer group in the south was to link up via Kolomna with the northern pincer, east of Moscow. The grinding worked, for a time, and officers with binoculars could see the sun, as it went down, glinting in the distance off the golden cupolas of the Kremlin buildings. Just close to Moscow, the Germans reached Krasnaya Polyana, Leo Tolstoy's estate, little more than ten miles away, but Tula itself still held, so that Guderian never got close to Moscow on that side. Because of the resistance on both the northern and southern sides of Moscow, Bock tried a direct attack from the west, but with few tanks, it ran out of steam four days later. There is today on the way to the Moscow airport a memorial at Khimki, which was a huge tank-trap. That was the Germans' limit, fifteen miles from the Kremlin. On 5 December 1941, fresh Soviet Siberian troops, prepared for winter warfare, attacked the German forces in front of Moscow. These substantial reinforcements had been sent west once it was clear that the Japanese were going to honour their undertaking to the Soviets rather than their undertaking to Hitler—one of the war's critical decisions. But these reserves had been carefully preserved elsewhere as well, and the Moscow campaign was over. By January 1942, the Soviets had driven the Germans back 200 miles in places, and the Germans were clearly too weak. They had lost three-quarters of a million men, not in the main replaced. When at Rostov in the south a Soviet counterattack on 30 November threatened encirclement, the commander of the Southern Army Group, Rundstedt, withdrew to the Mius and Donets rivers, a position later to become celebrated; the Germans were on the defensive all along the enormous line. On the northern front they were forced back from Tikhvin on the southern shore of Lake Ladoga, and a very narrow link was thus open to Leningrad.

The German position was terrible as the hard winter began. The existing Soviet rail system, in poor repair to start with, functioned very inefficiently. The oil used to grease the Schmeisser submachine guns froze. German winter uniforms had been left behind in Poland so as not to take up vital space, and on 20 December Goebbels appealed to the German people to send warm clothing to the soldiers. The day before, Hitler relieved the commander of the army, Field Marshal Walther von Brauchitsch, of his duties. He blamed Brauchitsch for failing to take Moscow. Henceforth the High Command of the Army would run the Russian war from Zossen, outside Berlin, at Hitler's direction. The Germans had almost reached the Caucasus, and they had cracked their way into the Crimea as well. The entry to the northern Caucasus and much of the northeastern coast of the Crimea were also now in German hands. However, the supply lines reaching these, in winter, were terrible, and the Soviet navy controlled the Black Sea so that even a sea route from Constanţa in Rumania could not work well for the Germans. And now the Russians managed a Dunkirk type of evacuation from Odessa to Sevastopol in the western Crimea. For all of the gigantic advances on the map, the Germans were in deadly danger, and some of the generals suggested pulling all the way back to Poland. But that was not Hitler's style. Maybe he guessed that if a retreat started, it would in the first place be hideously difficult—even worse than Napoleon's, which had anyway started in October—and would lead to panic. He ordered the troops to hold on where they were, in fortified positions, hedgehogs, that could be supplied from the air. The Russians attacked these again and again, with local successes, but the outcome proved Hitler right—the pockets indeed held on and cost the Russians a great deal. In the spring the Germans were still well forward, encircling Leningrad, threatening Moscow from Rzhev, only a hundred miles away, and then holding a line roughly along the river Dniepr, with its vast stretch to the east, and into the Crimea. There was going to be an enormous battle of worldwide dimensions.

WORLD WAR TWO

chapter four | PEARL HARBOR AND NORTH AFRICA

*preceding page: New Zealand troops in the Western Desert,
December 1941 (Bettmann/Corbis)*

The astounding German reverse before Moscow coincided almost exactly with another grand collision a hemisphere away. Out of the blue, the Japanese made a spectacular attack on the American base in the central Pacific, Pearl Harbor, in Hawaii. This had long origins: Japan had been the first non-European state to defeat a European navy, the Russian in 1904, and she now in turn thought in terms of running an empire. Although she had no raw materials, she had clever adaptability and had taken over many western markets in Asia. Later, during the Great Depression, Japan's giant neighbour, China, disintegrated, with a three-cornered fight between Japanese, Communists, and Republican Nationalists. The Japanese had occupied Peking and the trading ports, incurring the hostility of the United States, for which the Open Door Policy (free trade and non-intervention) was a cardinal rule, and one reason for the stiffness of the American response was the harshness of Japanese behaviour in China— master-race stuff, itself in imitation of the practices of certain European nations. Japanese brutality became notorious, and the

5,000 American missionaries reported back on it (Pearl Buck, a missionary's daughter whose novels sentimentalized Chinese peasant life, got a somewhat questionable Nobel Prize for Literature). The Japanese would brook no criticism, and the Americans threatened sanctions. Oil was Japan's great weak point, and in 1940, profiting from the collapse of France and Holland, Japanese troops moved into French Indochina and towards the oil-rich Dutch East Indies (now Indonesia). The result was tremendous hostility between Japan and both Great Britain and the United States, both of which imposed an oil embargo and froze Japanese assets. Given the Soviet-Japanese non-aggression pact, Japanese war plans went ahead, to disable the US Navy at Pearl Harbor, seize the islands of Guam and Wake, take the oil of the Dutch East Indies and the Philippines (a US territory since 1898), and expel the British from their naval base at Singapore. Then a Japanese Commonwealth (bizarrely rendered as a 'Co-Prosperity Sphere') would be established, and the West would not be able to interfere. Of course the Japanese, some of whose leaders knew the United States and Great Britain directly, understood that they themselves could be crushed, but they saw no alternative, given their extraordinary tradition of racial pride and their emperor's god-like status, and thought that there might just be a slender chance of victory.

On 7 December 1941 Japan hit Pearl Harbor with a brilliantly executed surprise attack. She was much aided, however, by the somnolescence with which the base had been run—aircraft neatly lined up on the ground to be bombed, anti-aircraft guns unmanned, the ammunition depots locked, the keys themselves hidden. It was fortunate that all three of the American aircraft carriers had been sent out, to guard another island that could be used for aircraft, but otherwise much damage was done, with eight American battleships out of action, and 2,402 Americans were killed. The Japanese had gambled that the United States, when faced with such a sudden and massive defeat, would agree to a negotiated settlement and allow Japan free rein in China. Naval Marshal General Isoroku Yamamoto himself, hero of the hour, did not think that the attack was the right thing to do— he knew the Americans and understood that, beyond initial muddle and bewilderment, they would fight back, would never forgive the humiliation. In any case American losses were less serious than initially thought: the American aircraft carriers were far more important than the battleships, and vital naval infrastructure (fuel oil tanks and the shipyard facilities), submarines, and signals intelligence units went unscathed because the Japanese, seeing the aircraft carriers were not there, feared a counter-strike and withdrew too soon.

The first six months of 1942 saw further American and British disasters in the Pacific. Churchill was an old imperialist, determined on a show of strength. He knew the importance of 'face' in upholding the Asian empire, the extraordinary and often un-reflecting self-confidence that went into running an Indian Raj of 400,000,000 souls with 60,000 British and a mainly native army. He ordered two warships to the Indian Ocean as a demonstration of might, but they were attacked from the air and these grand ships were sunk. The Japanese now used Thailand and Indochina for the invasion of Malaya, and the American air bases of Guam and Wake also fell to naval attack. On 1 January 1942 a Declaration by United Nations (the first time the term was used) set up a British-controlled supreme command in Southeast Asia, but the Japanese swept it aside, taking Manila in the Philippines and much of New Guinea. The grand catastrophe occurred on 15 February 1942, with the fall of Singapore. For more than a century Singapore had been a British possession, a lucrative centre of trade. When the Japanese invaded it on 8 February, it had 130,000 British imperial troops to defend it, five times more than the invading Japanese, but there were no British tanks against 200 Japanese tanks, and Japanese air superiority was overwhelming. After the surrender, some 80,000 prisoners of war—British, Australian, Indian—were marched off to a very cruel fate, of forced labour and starvation.

Then in late February and early March 1942, the Japanese navy swept all before it, and launched a raid into the Indian Ocean with attacks on Ceylon. A British aircraft carrier was sunk and British ships were prudently kept well away from the Indian Ocean. The Japanese also invaded Burma. The point of this move was to cut the supply line to the Nationalist Chinese, who had thwarted Japanese plans, and were still holding out. The Americans helped with military advisers, aircraft, and supplies carted along the Burma Road. The British initially meant to hold on to their colony, but there were too few troops, the Burmese were unreliable, and the Japanese, in 1942, had command of the air. They compelled the British to retreat—a thousand-mile trudge through very difficult terrain, which came to an end early in May at the Indian border, when the monsoon began and prevented any further Japanese progress. The Nationalist Chinese were now cut off, except for an extraordinarily hazardous supply line by air across the Himalayas. They nevertheless managed to hold down some three-fifths of the Japanese army: as Antony Beevor correctly writes, 'The Sino-Japanese conflict has long been like a missing section in the jigsaw of the Second World War.' Elsewhere there was no holding the Japanese tide. The best-known US general, Douglas MacArthur, said he would hold the Philippines, but his aircraft were mainly destroyed on the ground, and in March MacArthur was told to leave. He had retired from the army in 1937 to become military adviser to the Commonwealth Government of the Philippines, and was recalled to active duty in 1941. Now he slipped away to Australia, but famously promised 'I shall return.' His 80,000 men held out until 8 May at the island of Corregidor in Manila Bay. In Australia there was much nervousness at the sudden collapse of the American and European empires. Japan, an offshore island nation, had expanded over a huge area, her troops running large parts of China, threatening India, and her navy controlling a vast extent of sea, with Pacific islands as bases and strong points. Rabaul, off New Guinea, was built up as the chief naval base, but the Japanese also spread out across the Solomon Islands, with an airfield planned on Guadalcanal, and they used the captured American islands of Guam and Wake with effect.

The British were in a very exposed position. Their rule in India was obviously coming to an end, but they could neither walk away from her nor defend her adequately. Once their prestige had been broken, at Singapore and elsewhere, India became difficult to govern. The effort to resist Japan meant that the war effort elsewhere was weakened, and the worst British disasters occurred as 1942 went ahead. The fact was that the British had taken on far too much. Their empire was an extraordinary anomaly: how could an island off northwestern Europe conceivably manage a quarter of the world's land surface? Such a task was not possible without American support, and it was on this that Churchill gambled. The Pearl Harbor attack opened up America to the British war effort. America had been resisting entering another global conflict, and Congress had enacted several Neutrality Acts in the 1930s forbidding sales of arms to belligerents, but in December 1940, with Hitler's invasion of Poland in mind, President Roosevelt declared that America would become the 'arsenal of democracy'. His goal was to help Britain without entering the war. He devised Lend-Lease and Congress passed an authorization bill in March 1941 allowing the government to 'sell, transfer title to, exchange, lease, lend, or otherwise dispose of . . . any defense article' to specific nations, Britain being the first in March, China the second in April, and the Soviet Union the third in October. And then America entered the war in December. The first goal of the Allies now was to control the Atlantic and enable American troops and supplies to cross. By July 1942, as the Americans at last organized convoys in home waters, naval commander Karl Dönitz focused his U-boats on the North Atlantic. There were enough of them to form a long line, and sometimes up to fifteen boats would attack. Allied fighters could fly west from British bases or east from America to protect the convoys from U-boats; of course the planes had to husband their fuel, and always have enough to return to home base. Fighters at the time had enough fuel to protect only partway the journey of the convoys, and left unprotected was an area called the Mid-Atlantic Gap. It was here where the Allied convoys were most vulnerable and where most U-boat attacks occurred. In October 1942 alone, fifty-six ships, in all 250,000 tons, were sunk between Greenland and Iceland, in an area not covered by Allied aircraft. But on the other hand many more U-boats were also sunk—sixty in August–September, one for every ten merchant ships sunk, as against one for every forty previously. British Admiral Max Horton, the commander in chief of Western Approaches, the rectangular area projecting far into the Atlantic from the western coast of Great Britain, organized escorts as reserves, detached where necessary to hunt submarines, and he would have done better if there had been more planes at his disposal. There were new tactics—escorts would stay above a submarine for so long that its air would give out. The older depth charges were clumsy, and muddled the waters, but they were replaced often enough by hedgehog anti-submarine mortars that exploded on contact, while squid mortars had longer range (together they knocked out a quarter of the U-boats). Then came another ingenious invention, the Leigh Light. It was automatically switched on at night as soon as an aircraft made radar contact with a submarine on the surface (where it could move much faster and recharge its batteries), and it illuminated the target. The submarines were attacked out of the blue, and were sunk. The same result came from centimetric radar, which could be carried on an aircraft and was undetectable by the victim, which would be destroyed utterly unexpectedly.

For a ten-month period from February 1942, British code-breakers were defeated by upgrading of the Enigma machine. The U-boats proceeded largely undetected. The Germans were reading the British naval ciphers and knew the whereabouts of convoys, but the British could not read the German equivalents. The break for the Allies came on 30 October 1942, when, with great panache, British seamen seized a U-boat that had surfaced in the eastern Mediterranean, went aboard the wrecked vessel, and took off what they could find. What they retrieved helped change the course of the war. They found the new Enigma keys and code books that the Germans used to encipher their messages. Soon because Enigma had been cracked (the code broken by Alan Turing, that wizard with early computing), the British Admiralty could plot the U-boats' positions, allowing the Atlantic convoys carrying supplies from North America to Britain and the Soviet Union to get through unscathed. By December 1942 losses were much lower, and winter weather arrived as well. But in the spring the convoy battles began again, and there were so many submarines on patrol that convoys could hardly escape detection. In March, eighty-two ships were sunk in the Atlantic (476,000 tons) for the loss of twelve U-boats. For a time the British faced a severe supply problem, but then things changed—in April, only thirty-nine ships (235,000 tons) went down, but fifteen U-boats were lost and in May there was a dramatic turnaround, a battle over a slow convoy, Outbound (North) Slow ONS5, made up of forty-three merchantmen escorted by sixteen warships, and attacked by thirty U-boats. Thirteen merchant ships were lost, partly because a storm scattered the convoy, but six U-boats were sunk by escorts or aircraft; Slow Convoy SC130 saw five U-boats destroyed for no loss. In all in May, forty-three U-boats were destroyed, thirty-four in the Atlantic—twenty-five percent of the operational strength. The Allies lost thirty-four ships (134,000 tons). The prime reason for this was that the Mid-Atlantic Gap was closed by new planes, B-24 Liberators, that could travel far longer distances, and also by merchant or escort aircraft carriers that sailed with the convoys. Portugal allowed the Allies to use aircraft facilities in the Azores, and the RAF Coastal Command was to sink more U-boats than any other Allied service in the last three years of the war (after April 1942). In 1943, there were 258 U-boats lost, 90 sunk by Coastal Command, and 51 damaged. This meant that England could now plausibly be used for an American invasion of western Europe, which Stalin had been demanding for some time.

The years 1941 and 1942 saw downs and ups for the Allies. In Southeast Asia, the British position was collapsing, and the entire global strategic position seemed desperate except in North Africa. There, British forces were building a railway through a thousand miles of bleak desert between El Alamein near Alexandria and Tobruk in Libya. On 22 January 1941 they freed the fortress of Tobruk, which had been held by Italy. But then they ran into problems of supply, even of water, and the Italians and Germans counter-attacked. The British Eighth Army prepared an attack, Operation Battleaxe, into the eastern Libyan region of Cyrenaica, which includes Tobruk. Battleaxe forces included 100,000 men, 849 tanks, and 604 aircraft, against somewhat less. The British had laid down elaborate minefields to channel any Panzer attack, and good new equipment was coming in— Grant tanks, with armour and a gun that could withstand Panzer IVs instead of being out-ranged (the six-pounder gun matched the Germans' 50-mm Pak 38).

Erwin Rommel, the Desert Fox, was the great adversary of the Allies in North Africa. He had charisma, was adored by his men, and even managed to disarm the greatest British weapon, Ultra. He disobeyed instructions from the High Command in Rome and took British Intelligence entirely by surprise; at the same time, he could read the local radio traffic in North Africa, and so he knew what to do. On 26 May 1942 he found a weak spot, and even overran the headquarters of an armoured division. British armoured brigades came into action one by one, without the support of anti-tank guns or motorized infantry that the Germans had. Rommel had also ingeniously used the British minefields, and had a screen of anti-tank guns that covered his engineers disabling the minefields. Meanwhile, the British general Neil Ritchie, a good staff officer, commanded in slow motion and units fought without coordination, each being defeated in turn. Coming round the southern flank with a flanking manoeuvre into the desert, Rommel trapped the static British against their own minefields. On the southern side the Free French gave a very good account of themselves at Bir Hakeim, a sign (remembered as a Metro station in Paris) that the French were recovering. But Rommel got through, and the Panzers attacked on three sides, leaving a litter of damaged tanks that the British would have done well to salvage but did not. The Eighth Army fell back on the Egyptian border, leaving Tobruk isolated. The fortress had been weakened, its mines removed to set up the fortified positions, or boxes, on which the British depended. Columns of dust, relentless bombing, and troops' inexperience meant that the place collapsed, leaving huge quantities of supplies and 35,000 prisoners (21 June). Churchill was gently told in Washington by Roosevelt, who offered immediate help. The American attaché in Cairo sent devastating reports of British inefficiency, and the Italians could read his code: in the circumstances Rommel girded himself for a further push—this time with enormous help from the captured vehicles and fuel.

After the fall of Tobruk in June 1942, there was another mauling on the Egyptian border. The British were now down to a hundred tanks, having lost half of their artillery. Even now, textbook nerveless prudence reigned as far as defensive systems were concerned, and troops were placed, static, in their boxes, defended by minefields that Rommel could just bypass. But the British were learning, and their commander, Sir Claude Auchinleck, imposed himself, at last replacing a man whom he shrank, out of decency, from dismissing, to make the troops mobile. He was too late and there was another muddle, after which Auchinleck, a field marshal, was photographed standing disconsolately and alone in his baggy shorts by the side of the road as his army retreated to the nearest convenient defensible point. Here, the British Army's learning curve went up. It was at the railway station in the Mediterranean town of El Alamein (meaning 'The

Two Flags', British and Egyptian). El Alamein was the narrowest front on which to stand, some forty miles of scrubby desert with two slight rises that went by the name 'ridge', permitting observation and, of a sort, cover. The desert came to an end at a huge depression, an area of salt marshes, useless for military or any other purposes. It could only be out-flanked to the south, but that was the Sahara Desert, itself unusable by tanks. The Alamein position already had fortified boxes, the most developed round the railway station, festooned with barbed wire. There was now an atmosphere of panic as the British fleet moved from Alexandria and the headquarters staff burned their papers. Mussolini groomed a white horse for his entry to Cairo, and on 30 June, Rommel approached the Alamein position. But his men were very tired, and had had their own losses; water was a problem. Auchinleck had scraped together an Indian brigade from Iraq, with better anti-tank guns, and the RAF established air superiority. Soon, Rommel was down to thirty-seven tanks, and his three German divisions counted under 2,000 men each. Besides, his supplies from Italy were now seriously curtailed—5,000 tons in June and July as against 34,000 in May. The frontier battle petered out, and a counter-attack led to the capture of one of Rommel's main assets, his signals interceptors.

All during the North African campaign Churchill had been a great nuisance. He sent peremptory cables, demanding action and victory at a time when the field commanders had to wrestle with endless difficulties. Finally he came to Cairo, and sacked Auchinleck; the eventual successor, Bernard Montgomery, Monty, was peppery, vain, and a man for endless detail. He took trouble to make himself known to the men, and he even overawed Churchill, who accepted a degree of care and preparation that he would not have tolerated in Montgomery's predecessors— asking for which, indeed, had caused their dismissals. Montgomery also had enormous superiority in men and materiel, but he took his time, waiting until the supply lines functioned properly, and air superiority could be built up. Still, a considerable British victory was at last forthcoming.

The Alamein position, however, now favoured Rommel's defence, though he had far fewer tanks and aircraft than Montgomery. He laid minefields with half a million mines, some lifted from Tobruk. The Italians were masters of the dummy minefield as well. There was no chance of a flanking envelopment, attacking the sides of the enemy, then enveloping him, so there would have to be a breakthrough. Still, with 220,000 men and 1,100 tanks, Montgomery had enormous superiority to Rommel, with his 115,000 men and 559 tanks. Much ingenuity was displayed in dummy tanks (jeeps disguised with painted boxwood) and other matters, but the essentials were absolute command of the air and the steady interruption of German-Italian supply lines. It also helped that Rommel, worn down by strain, was sick. Montgomery meant to cut passages through the minefields in the north, sending in the sappers to clear these corridors with fast-working Polish-designed mine detectors. Each passage would be wide enough for one tank, and a great bombardment, as in 1916, would smash all before it. This, with almost 1,000 guns, opened on 23 October, and lasted for six hours, each gun firing 600 rounds. Then the infantry went in, with sappers, who found that their job was beyond them—the minefields were five miles thick. If a single tank broke down, or its engine was affected by sand and dust, the whole column would be halted, a sitting target for German anti-tank guns, of which the 88-mm were greatly feared, for their range and penetration. Attacking the weaker (but not hopeless) Italians, the British did make some progress, but generally the first efforts failed. Rommel, ill, was convalescing, and now the one advantage was that his stand-in had a heart attack and died, leaving the German command empty. Rommel, still not well, returned. Now the guns and aircraft—a thousand sorties (i.e., single-plane lift-offs) by the RAF—did their work in grinding down the Germans and Italians, dropping 135 tons of explosive, but no breakthrough happened. Montgomery switched his main attack on the northern side, to cut off the German-Italian line as it jutted out towards El Alamein. Australians and Scottish Highlanders ground away, and Rommel had neither the reserves nor the fuel for an effective counter-attack.

Montgomery was stuck by 26 October, and Churchill held his head in his hands: 'Is it really impossible to find a general who can win a battle?' But the RAF came to the rescue. The last German tanker was sunk, at the port of Tobruk, and Montgomery, thinning his front line, created a reserve with which to launch another attack. The battlefield was now hellish—a heat haze, in which flies gathered in huge black clouds over corpses, the wounded, excrement, with shattered guns and burning trucks or tanks—and the British were better able to take the grinding than the Germans. By 29 October, they had 800 tanks, to 148 German and 187 Italian, which were hardly mobile. A tanker was torpedoed from the air off Greece, and two more were sunk off Tobruk on 1 November. Rommel knew that it would not be easy even to pull back: he would have to stay put and fight where he was. Montgomery switched and turned up the pressure on the northern side, with seven hours of aerial bombing followed by four hours of bombardment from 360 guns. Now the engineers, fully protected, could clear five ways through minefields, and though an attack on an anti-tank gun screen beyond the Alamein station caused total loss of an armoured brigade, the Germans' losses were proportionately more. They had at most thirty-five tanks ready, and the artillery had come down to one-third strength. Rommel told Hitler he must withdraw, was told not to, held on, and then faced 400 tons of bombs, dropped in 1,208 aircraft sorties on 3 November. Rommel retreated: he explained later, 'There were no reserves, as every available man and gun had been put into the line. So now it had come, the thing we had done everything in our power to avoid—our front broken and the fully motorised enemy streaming into our rear. Superior orders could no longer count. We had to save what there was to be saved.' His deputy was captured. On 4 November Montgomery broke through, but still behaved with prudence, and no doubt remembered how, as the British had advanced over this terrain in the past, they had been given a bloody surprise by Rommel's resilience. But the Germans were now broken, and down to 5,000 men, twenty tanks, and fifty guns. They retreated skilfully a thousand miles, to Tunisia.

In England on 15 November the church bells rang. They had been silent since 1940 because they were meant to announce a

German invasion. Now that was ruled out, and British public opinion was at last handed a victory. Churchill addressed the nation: 'Rommel's army has been defeated. It has been routed. It has been very largely destroyed as a fighting force.' With the insight of the practicing historian that he was, he put the victory into context: 'Now this is not the end. It is not even the beginning of the end. But it is, perhaps, the end of the beginning.' Later after the war, Churchill would write, 'Before Alamein we never had a victory. After Alamein, we never had a defeat.'

For the British towards the end of 1942, the most important events were at sea and in the air. If the Atlantic had been semi-closed, then they would have been helpless, and if the Germans had maintained their superiority in the air, then the Russians would also have been helpless, unable to hold the Germans. The key to both of these was British. It was true that in North Africa only three German divisions were involved, at that one of them classed as 'Light', while the rest were Italian. But what was at stake in North Africa was enormous—the Middle East, its oil, its strategic connections.

The problem was that, as the war had developed, not just the British, but also the Americans, had been enormously diverted. Perhaps the central difficulty lay in General O'Connor's very early victory over the Italians, in 1940. That cheered up the British, and when the North African campaign went wrong, at the turn of 1941–42, there were already troops there, in Egypt, and the obvious move was to reinforce them. That again had a ratchet effect, and the main British land effort was in a part of the world the Americans regarded as either sinister—a matter of imperialism—or irrelevant. But then the British lost, and the situation needed to be retrieved. One obvious way was for an Anglo-American force to conquer French North Africa, and thereby finish Rommel off from the west, given that he had not been finished off from the east. For the Americans, the alternative was to concentrate against Japan, in the Pacific. It is a mark of Roosevelt's statesmanship that he kept to the Atlantic First formula; he would have been even more popular at home had he concentrated on the Pacific.

It made sense for the Americans, as their forces grew, to intervene in North Africa, not elsewhere, and Churchill had sold them the idea. Operation Torch was conceived—the transport of an enormous Anglo-American force to French North Africa (*torcher* in French means 'to wipe a bottom'). There was curiously enough a Polish intelligence network in Casablanca, as in the film, though the actor there was Viennese, and there were secret contacts with the local Vichy authorities in October. A French general, Henri Giraud, a very brave man but not bright, was smuggled out of Vichy France to be the Allies' man (he wanted to be commander in chief and withdrew when that was refused). The Allies planned three task forces for amphibious landings to seize the key ports and airports and then move east to Tunis and Rommel's rear. It was an extraordinary success, given the circumstances. General George Patton with 35,000 men, at Casablanca in Morocco, had come from the United States in a hundred ships; other, Anglo-American, troops had come mainly from Glasgow to land in Algeria after passing through the Straits of Gibraltar. The U-boats in the area were drawn off to attack a mercantile convoy, and on 8 November Patton landed. There was some resistance, some of the men of Vichy being violently hostile to the British in particular. They were in the end defeated because one of the biggest figures of Vichy, Admiral François Darlan, happened to be there, and told them to give in. Darlan was a much-compromised figure, who had even allowed Rommel to employ French supply routes, and for the Allies to be seen using him looked questionable. The leader of the Free French, Charles de Gaulle, of course had no time for him or, for that matter, for Giraud; de Gaulle's huge advantage was that he could work with the largely Communist resistance inside France, and it was highly convenient for him when Darlan was assassinated (in mysterious circumstances, by a very young man who, in turn, was speedily judicially murdered before he could talk).

Though with much blundering and clumsiness, the British and Americans were in Rommel's rear. There was a further advantage, in that French troops (in effect Moroccan or Algerian) were again in the war. Churchill and Roosevelt now met triumphally, at Casablanca, and their forces invaded Tunisia in January, just as Rommel arrived. There was an initial embarrassment, with inexperienced American troops, at the battle of Kasserine Pass, in February, where the Desert Fox showed his old panache, but of course the Allies were overwhelmingly strong, and had complete control both of sea and air. There followed an absurd episode, when Hitler poured German troops into this hopeless position, and in May some 250,000, almost half of them German, became prisoners of war. Hitler's move seems senseless, but it had the odd and maybe foreseen side effect, that the invading season was now so far advanced that there could be no invasion of France in 1943. There are more imponderables about Torch itself. All of this had been designed to help the British in Egypt, and it would maybe have been better if Montgomery had just not fought at El Alamein at all, because Rommel's communications to the west were under threat and he would have had in any event to withdraw. Seen from Moscow (and even from Washington) this whole campaign was an imperialist side show, and Stalin might even have thought that the British were making Russians die in millions in order to protect their own position in the Middle East. But Torch had grown out of Tobruk, and Tobruk had grown out of Mussolini's involvement in June 1940. Hundreds of thousands of men, with hundreds of ships, were now in North Africa because of a war that had begun in Poland. What were they to do next? The answer, not much liked by the Americans, was Italy. It was too late in the season for France. There would in other words be a further period when, on land, the Russians would be on their own.

chapter five | THE RUSSIAN TURN-AROUND

preceding page: Friedrich von Paulus after surrendering at Stalingrad, February 1943 (Georges de Keerle/Sygma/Corbis)

Adolf Hitler's last moment of military inspiration had been his insistence on holding the line in Russia. The Red Army had squandered its resources on bull-headed attacks in the snows, and though the Germans had been driven back, they held out in pockets that were supplied from the air. As the spring 1941 thaw immobilized everything in slush and mud and flood, the front line zig-zagged, with deep bends, from Leningrad to a long finger, the Rzhev salient, pointing at Moscow, and then southeast, past Kharkov, the second city of the Ukraine, roughly along the Donets to the Crimea. There, in December 1941, the Russians had regained the Kerch peninsula on the northeastern shore, at the mouth of the Sea of Azov. Both sides had wounds to lick, and the Germans faced endless problems. They had lost over a hundred officers every day, their casualties ran to 1,100,000, and sickness, since November 1941, had cost them 600,000. Seventy-four thousand motor vehicles had just broken down, and only a third of the anyway inadequate railway network had been adapted to take German rolling stock. Of this limited capacity, eleven trains per day carried petrol, but the army depended on horses, and they too presented problems—180,000 had dropped dead in the winter.

The Germans were of course attempting far too much, and their war economy was not prepared for a long ordeal. Where were priorities to be set—navy? Long-range heavy bombers? Fighters? Very heavy tanks? And how was occupied Europe to be exploited? In 1941 these matters were hardly sorted out at all, and Germany went on producing ordinary consumption goods at prewar levels (themselves of course not, by British—let alone American—standards, high). In the Messerschmitt factory in southern Bavaria, for example, aluminium was misallocated to make ladders for civilian use, while the British were already using it to lighten their fighters and give them a longer range. But the greatest problem concerned oil. Germany relied on the oil she got from Rumania, and otherwise the very expensive synthetic fuel derived from lignite (brown coal), at the Leuna works near Leipzig and other refineries. In the end this problem would break the German war effort, and by 1945 it would be immobilized. The Russians, by contrast, got enormous quantities from the southern Caucasus, where the output of the Baku oil wells was moved, via Astrakhan on the Caspian, along the Volga. The British were also extremely well-supplied, from Iran especially for the African and Far Eastern campaigns. Now in 1942 Hitler decided that he must have that oil, for as he said, without it, the war was lost. In fact, as it turned out, 1942 would present the last moment when he could act: in 1943, British bombing, hitherto largely ineffectual, would pose a deadly threat and force the Luftwaffe away from the eastern front and towards the defence of Germany's cities. The Luftwaffe, itself a hot-house growth from the 1930's, was forced to take on more than its structure could stand, and it had neither sufficient fighters nor suitable bombers. Now, starting in June 1942, a prodigious operation was going to be mounted, called *Fall Blau* (Case Blue), for Prussia's colour. It was a gamble, but as so often happened, Hitler's enemies gave him enormous help.

The victory at the last minute before Hitler reached Moscow had gone to Stalin's head. He had had one great moment, when he refused to leave Moscow and held the anniversary parade of the Revolution in Red Square, with the Germans very close; he assumed they would now collapse. They had after all had to fall back some way, having lost Rostov in the south and, to the east of Leningrad, an important town on the railway line that kept the city going, Tikhvin. Efforts to relieve Leningrad dominated everything in that area, as the only way to the stricken city was across the ice of Lake Ladoga, an inland sea into which the river Volkhov flowed, near Tikhvin. That winter was a terrible experience for the city, as hundreds of thousands of people starved and froze. The exiguous supply line across the ice, already inadequate for the city's supply, had also to be used to evacuate Leningrad's industrial machinery, vital for the war economy.

From January to June 1942, the Leningrad and Volkhov Army Groups were pushed again and again into action. The Germans had nothing to match the Soviet T-34 tanks, which could manoeuvre on the frozen swamp-soil, and they fell back, but when the weather improved, the Germans attacked at the initial point of Soviet breakthrough, and sealed the attackers in a pocket, now swampy and mosquito-infested. Their commander, Andrey Vlasov, a very ambitious man who had been moved in at the last minute, was given hopeless instructions, landed in a muddle, and by 25 June 60,000 of his men had been lost. Vlasov himself was captured by the Germans, switched sides, tried to raise a Russian Liberation Movement for his captors, and was executed by the Soviets after the war.

There was a bigger disaster still in the Crimea. The naval fortress of Sevastopol, on the western shore, was under siege, and the Red Army, on the eastern one, was to strike out to relieve it. Clumsy efforts were made from February to April, with high losses, and the Germans, with control of the air, did much damage to the Soviet supply ships. Then on 8 May, Erich von Manstein, commander of the Eleventh Army in the Crimea, launched a well-prepared operation to clear the Kerch peninsula. It meant a frontal attack, but one so ingeniously staged that the bulk of the Russian forces were placed on the wrong wing, and then surrounded. The Germans took 170,000 men, with 258 tanks and 1,100 guns, and in June 1942, in a month-long murderous epic, Sevastopol itself was taken, though in ruins, with 95,000 prisoners. The taking of Sevastopol coincided with the fall of Tobruk. But the worst of all was to come.

The Eastern Front was marked by wide, long rivers. The Dniepr, in its course, bellied out from Kiev far to the southeast before flowing into the Black Sea; the Northern Donets flowing through Kharkov, and into the Donets, bellied out to the east; the Don, after another southeasterly bend, curved back through Rostov to the Sea of Azov. Beyond these was the greatest river of all, the Volga, flowing into the oil-rich Caspian. The Red Army in its January attacks towards Kharkov had established a bridgehead over the Donets River, around Izyum. Kharkov and the railway link lay only forty miles behind the lines, and the Izyum salient would have to be cleared if *Blau* was to go ahead at all. Matters were further complicated in that the Red Army in March had established another but shallower bridgehead over the Donets, north of Izyum. Stalin encouraged his front-line commander, Semyon Timoshenko, with grandiose plans, and there was a further attack from the tip of the salient with 540,000 men, 1,200 tanks, 10,000 guns, and 900 aircraft. The stated aim was to take 'important crossing-points over the Dniepr', a hundred miles southwest of Kharkov. This got going on 12 May, and the Red Army was close to Kharkov. The Germans responded boldly, letting Timoshenko drive forward, after which Kleist's Panzer group attacked, with total surprise, far in his rear and with a whole flying corps (500 planes) in support. Timoshenko weakened his Kharkov attack, was trapped by 22–23 May, and when fuel reserves gave out on 26th, in the pocket, his forces collapsed—22 divisions, 15 tank brigades, 7 cavalry divisions, with 540 aircraft, over 1,200 tanks, and 2,000 guns being lost. Two hundred and forty thousand prisoners marched off. There was a further German attack on the northern bridgehead (Volchansk), which took 21,000 prisoners by 15 June. Now it was the Germans' turn to move forward across the steppe, this time with a six-to-one superiority in tanks, where previously the Russians had had a three-to-one advantage. On 28 June, *Blau* went ahead, along the Don. There was a Soviet bridgehead at Voronezh, which worried Bock, because the Red Army would be on his open flank if this was not dealt with. Hitler wanted him just to plunge straight on, as fast as possible, and a row developed. In fact the Russians were learning just to retreat, while building up their forces in the rear, and by 7 July it was clear that the Russians were extracting themselves from Bock's attack. The real problem was that there just were not enough mobile forces, and in any case they were not, given fuel problems, very mobile. Argument at Hitler's summer headquarters in the Ukrainian city of Vinnitsa turned poisonous. The generals argued with Hitler as to who had said what when. To document these things in future, every word said in the headquarters huts, air-conditioning clanking, mosquitoes buzzing, was taken down by shorthand writers—not encouraging for the trust that military operations need. But there was not as yet much Soviet resistance, and the Germans divided their forces—Army Group A was set to invade the Caucasus and get the oil, while Army Group B stood guard on its northern flank, on the lower Volga. The Sixth Army, the spearhead, reached the eastern extremity of the bend of the river Don and crossed it in mid-August. A narrow land-bridge separated this from the Volga.

The chief city on the lower Volga was Stalingrad, an old town built up for Five-Year-Plan modern industry and, like others, re-named for revolutionary figures. The Red Army prepared for battle there, and set up a new army group, named after it, with 200,000 men, 400 tanks, over 2,000 guns, and 454 planes. The city was prepared, livestock and machinery transferred to the eastern side of the Volga, and Stalin, who had deceived himself that the real threat was to Moscow, now saw what was going on, as, on 23 July, the Germans took Rostov-on-Don. Motorized troops were to move on the Caspian at Astrakhan, but fuel supplies continued to be a problem: 1,500 tons went to the Don front in trucks attached to Army Group B, whose Sixth Army was delayed for a fatal week because of the fuel shortage. Besides, diversion of strength continued—some good units to the west, where a second front was now feared; a transfer of Manstein's command to Leningrad, where there were plans, not realized, of linking up with the Finns to enclose the city tightly. In the months that followed, the Leningrad attack could not be properly pursued because of distractions to the south, where the Red Army mounted powerful attacks—more powerful than was later said, given that they were defeated: a sharp-eyed American historian, David Glantz, disinterred these, and they showed the extraordinary inventiveness of one of the German generals, Walter Model, in holding the front line, at Rzhev and Gzhatsk, not far from Moscow, as it had been stabilized in spring 1942. Partisans were now a problem, as potatoes had to be picked under military supervision and there were five or six attacks every day in the area of Army Group Centre.

This was the crisis of the USSR in 1942. It had lost a good third of its industry, and two-fifths of its population were in German-occupied territory; the Donets Basin had supplied fifty-seven percent of its coal, and there was also vast loss in the ores needed for iron or copper or mercury or tin or lead, and phosphates, graphite, iodine; there were also signs of demoralisation in the army—for instance the collapse of the improvised defence line on the southern Don when Rostov fell. The Germans' advance from there went fast, in late July, as they crossed the Manych, the river that marks the boundary between Europe and Asia in that area. Army Group A was to move along the Black Sea coast towards Batum, and block Soviet naval bases, but it was also to take the oil town of Maikop, the capital of the Adygea District, and the oil wells (assuming both that the native peoples would collaborate and that the Red Army was dissolving—the army group alone had taken 309,000 prisoners from 1 July to 10 August). A Rumanian-German attack, with gliders, cleared the Taman Peninsula at the eastern edge of the mouth of the Sea of Azov, and the Germans did get into the port of Novorossiysk (it turned out to be their last serious prize, though they managed to hold onto it and the Kuban bridgehead for another year). Maikop fell on 9 August, but there were only four path-roads through the Caucasus, for mules, and even the field kitchens had to stay behind: the only vehicle of any use was the Kettenkrad, a sort of motorbike-tank. On 22 August skilled mountain troops planted a German flag on Mount Elbrus, which dominates the northern side of the Caucasus as Ararat does the southern side. The Germans got within twenty-five miles of the city of Sukhumi on the Black Sea coast, but by now they were so far from base that food took a week to arrive, and there were 2,000 mules too few. There were further bitter arguments in headquarters, the climax of weeks' tension about the army's cautiousness. Meanwhile at Maikop, the least of the oil fields, 6,500 experts arrived, hoping to extract 3,500,000 tons of oil, but they were attacked by partisans and the oil fields had been wrecked (they recovered in all only fifty barrels, and the engineers' quarters were blown up by ingenious partisans). The Germans were stuck, and Hitler went into a rage and even cut off social contact as he realized that he would not attain the objectives of the 1942 campaign. His rages became hurricane-force as he denounced the entire army and swore he could not wait to throw off his military jacket. The army had lost 200,000 men in August and only half could be replaced.

Up to 24 July the attack on the inner Don bend towards Kalach had gone well enough. On 30 July Hoth's 4th Panzer Army with a Rumanian corps came under Army Group B, as the Sixth Army (under Friedrich Paulus, the son of a schoolteacher; his wife was aristocratic Rumanian, a Rosetti-Solescu) was too weak in infantry for the attack on Stalingrad. It was very hot, and there was not much water in the steppe as the Germans marched forward. There was a sudden victory on 7 August on the approach to Kalach, west of Stalingrad: 57,000 prisoners, 1,000 tanks, 750 guns, and 650 planes, but it gave the Russians time; on 24 August Hoth's Panzer Army came up from the south, resistance weakened, and by early September the Germans were in the suburbs of Stalingrad. It was clear that the place was going to be stoutly defended.

Zhukov was appointed to Stalingrad on 26 August. He convinced Stalin not to stage just local counter-attacks and started planning a much larger counter-offensive against the weak German-Rumanian flanks, taking two months on the preparation. This was right: the five-hundred-mile Don flank was thinly covered by allies of questionable reliability: a Hungarian army weak in anti-tank guns, an Italian army that had marched 600 miles, and Rumanians, who counted as the best of these allied soldiers. On the day of Zhukov's flight to Moscow to explain his plans, Paulus saw Hitler in Vinnitsa to be given his fix of optimism (although even drinking water was scarce) and on 10 September the Panzer Corps reached the Volga just south of Stalingrad. The railway station on the northern side was taken on the 13th. The fighting then changed character. It was house to house, and feature to feature—the battles at the Mamayev Mound, the silo, the tractor factory, all of them entering history and film. Paulus complained of his troops' exhaustion, but Hitler on 6 October proclaimed the capture of Stalingrad the main task of the army group. There was maybe an argument that, though ruined, the place offered better protection for the coming winter than the open steppe, and Goering grandiosely promised aerial relief, but food supplies were not safe and transport lines were weak—three converted single-track ones for three armies leading back 1,500 miles to Germany, where there was already a jam of hundreds of trains. The average arrival at Sixth Army was four trains instead of the eight to ten needed. Roads—mud—were also a problem, and supplies heaped up immobilized in depots, while horses died in droves. But Hitler was caught on his own propaganda and had even said on 30 September that the worst was over, that the place would soon fall, and the orders multiplied. By mid-October the Germans had indeed reached the Volga, cutting the defence in two, but house-to-house battling exhausted the troops, and the vast air and artillery involvement was not as effective as it was supposed to be. Further Sixth Army attacks, on the gun factory and the metallurgical works, failed on the 17th.

Zhukov's counter-thrust, through the Don bridgeheads at Kletskaya and Bolshoy had been very well-prepared, for there were ambitions even to seize Rostov and trap the German Army Group A in the Caucasus. Great secrecy was observed, and troops moved at night: for the Volga bridgehead, in twenty days 160,000 men, 10,000 horses, 430 tanks, and 6,000 guns were freighted across. Reserves were intelligently created as troops were withdrawn from the front for rest and training. The Rumanians on the Don front had only a miscellany of captured (Czech etc.) artillery and their only reserve was a cavalry division almost without horses, while divisions each had some twelve miles to defend, with an unfavourable tactical lie. They were even expected to take over some of the Italian line. On the southern side, the Rumanian position was even worse—100,000 men for 150 miles and some of the line covered by observers. There were only thirty-four 7.5-cm anti-tank guns (and sixty on the Don) and only a sixth of the required mines had been given out. But though Hitler worried about the Don flank, he and even chief of the army staff general Franz Halder seem to have thought the Russians had been too greatly weakened. Intelligence was feeble, and Hitler went back from Vinnitsa on 7 November via Munich and the Berghof, his residence in the Bavarian Alps, to the Wolf's Lair, his Eastern Front military headquarters in the East Prussian town of Rastenburg, just as the great events of the year were unfolding. On 8 November, while Rommel was cracking at El Alamein, Hitler spoke at

Munich on the Nazi Party's anniversary, almost the last public address he was to make, and you can hear that voice making an effort to recover its former power, as it announces that Stalingrad has actually fallen. Retribution was only ten days away.

The Germans had no idea what was coming. Until the start, the great mass of Soviet tanks had remained concealed. On 19 November thirty divisions attacked the Rumanian Third Army, and its tanks had been dug in to protect them, because they were immobile for lack of fuel; but mice had eaten their electrical wire, and so they could not even fire. The Russians broke through, south, southeast, and southwest, and were twenty miles into the rear of the Sixth Army. A second attack came, on the next day, from the Volga beachhead south of the city, and it hit another Rumanian army; the two pincers closed on the Germans at Kalach on the Don. The German Panzer Corps opposite not only lacked fuel but was in tanks no stronger than a Panzer regiment, with some eighty tanks, while the weather prevented Air Fleet 4 from flying. On the 21st the northern attack reached the very headquarters of the Sixth Army, which had to flee, abandoning everything. Two German divisions west of the Don could not move for lack of fuel. Paulus knew there was a problem as regards supply by air to a fortified hedgehog, and prepared plans for a breakout. But Hitler forbade this, even though the army group command warned that it could not mount any relief attack (from Kotelnikovo, seventy miles southwest of Stalingrad) until 10 December, and Wolfram von Richthofen for the Luftwaffe said that any idea of air supply should be forgotten.

There was confusion in the German High Command. Hitler was on the move, others were in Salzburg; the new chief of the army staff, Kurt Zeitzler, was at Rastenburg (and to show Hitler what the men at Stalingrad were having to suffer, he ate the same rations as they had, and lost twenty-eight pounds in two weeks). The hope was that with the new Tiger tanks, and the example of the pockets that had held out in the previous winter, all would be well. Manstein was now named chief of a new Army Group Don. He was guaranteed twelve divisions, too few for the task, and the 179 aircraft were too dispersed, just doing routine tasks. With a twenty-mile advance over three days, the attack petered out by 19 December. The agony of Stalingrad now really began, and although Goering had promised air supply, the contribution was never enough and declined: the whole base infrastructure for aircraft—such as winter protection, weather stations, repair— was not there, and the Russians often knocked out aircraft scraped together, including training machines, with crews under great stress. The army was using 132 tons of ammunition every day, but the aircraft flew in little more than sixteen tons daily until 2 December and fifty-three after that; only a tenth of the fuel got through, and the horses died from lack of fodder. The men got only eleven ounces of bread a day, four ounces of meat (including horsemeat), and an ounce of fat. On the 16th, with the thermometer at −30 centigrade the men had horse soup and two slices of bread. Paulus himself said there was only enough until 18 December, though almost 500 tons were flown in 18–21 December, at the expense of freight room for ammunition. On the 21st Paulus reported the first deaths from starvation. With fuel only for a few miles, there was no hope of a successful breakout. Meanwhile the Russians built up their forces and shattered an Italian army (19 December) on the Don causing German Fourth Air Corps to disperse its strength on the Don attack; a landing place fell, with seventy planes lost and all their supplies. Up to 12 January, only 110 tons were flown in, some of it quite superfluous, whereas hardly two percent of the needed ammunition arrived. By 14 January the pocket had shrunk to a third of the earlier size and the main airport (Pitomnik) was lost, causing panic, as all the planes flew off. Still, on 25 January the Germans defiantly put up a swastika flag on the highest building that was left and even Paulus prattled on about 'fanatical will'. By 28 January the wounded and weaponless were simply given nothing, and when planes dropped supplies they now often fell into Russian hands. In the end a divisional commander, operating out of the Univermag department store, where what was left of Paulus's staff also stayed, showed the white flag, and the same happened at the tractor factory on the northern side, where junior commanders gave up.

Zhukov's aim had been to entrap Army Group A before it could pull out of the Caucasus. Such a withdrawal would have been extraordinarily difficult to bring off under any circumstances. Hitler wanted at least to keep Maikop, but the true imperative was to hold onto Rostov and to re-form Manstein's Army Group Don, to which Kleist's group in the Caucasus was subordinated. Two armies now had to retreat, trying, not always successfully, to take the equipment, while also scorching the earth. The army group of twenty divisions (400,000 men) was to pull back into a position on the eastern promontory of the Crimea, called Gotenkopf (Goth's Head: the Crimea had been a sort of reserve for the decendants of the ancient Germanic Goths, whose language survived to be recorded in the sixteenth century), and the retreat was mainly over by early February, with distances of 300 to 350 miles covered in winter conditions and without air protection. Via the Crimea, the troops that had escaped were sent to Manstein and to the middle Don, where an Army Group South (under Maximilian von Weichs) covered 200 miles with too few troops to protect Manstein's northern flank, once Stalingrad had surrendered. The Voronezh bridgehead was abandoned, but giving up the Don Basin was ruled out, because without its resources, said Paul Pleiger, the official in charge, the new tank programmes would not work. However, the threat to Manstein's western wing was very serious by the end of January, and he extracted troops with dexterity from the eastern wing (led by Maximilian Fretter-Pico and Karl-Adolf Hollidt) to cover Kharkov. Now the Russians managed to take Kursk in the west, early in February, and a hundred miles south developed a threat to Kharkov. Hitler had summoned the SS Panzerkorps, but by 9 February the emergency was general, as Belgorod and Izyum fell, and the SS commander disobeyed Hitler's orders so as to escape a Russian pincer. He withdrew from Kharkov on 16 February.

Hitler generally just ordered his generals not to retreat, but this was a desperate situation, and Manstein needed to be flexible. There was a gap between the two main army groups, on the river Dniepr, and the Russians were driving towards it, outrunning their supplies in jubilant over-confidence as they retook

Kharkov. Manstein scraped troops together from the crowded Gotenkopf position, and SS reinforcements arrived; and the Russians mistook these troop movements for a retreat. A well-organized attack northwards by the 1st Panzer Army (which had been extracted from the Crimea) struck the Russian flank and rear, such that Kharkov was retaken, and the line of the Donets recovered, in early March. Air Fleet 4 with nearly a thousand planes had been very effective with a thousand sorties per day. The overall position was as it had been in May 1942, and Kharkov had shown that, properly managed, German soldiers had a great deal of fight left. The Donets position, including Belgorod, was then re-occupied.

There were further problems in the north and centre. Just south of Lake Ladoga at Schlüsselburg the Germans had been able to threaten the remaining Russian link to Leningrad. There were miniature Stalingrads, ordeals of endurance, but by far the most important was the breaking of the Germans' blockade of Leningrad in January 1943. Lake Ladoga now had oil pipelines, and frost made the ground much more usable than in the summer (when the Volkhov front, east of the city, became marshy). The Red Army launched an attack on the narrow strip of land at Schlüsselburg that the Germans held on the southern edge of Lake Ladoga, between the Leningrad defenders and their would-be liberators to the east. His troops there were cut off and Hitler would not allow retreat. The Northern Army Group did not have reserves, for there were battles also on its southern side, where the long Demyansk salient, which had survived from the days of the initial advance on Moscow, threatened Rybinsk, the vast reservoir that supplied Moscow with water. The exposed Demyansk position was given up, though the larger one around Rzhev held out for another two months. But at enormous cost, there was at last, after 506 days, a land connection to Leningrad, even though it was only eight miles wide, and trains using it were within range of German guns. The Eastern Front was again in balance: could victory have been assured a year earlier, if the western Allies had staged a landing in France, instead of waiting until 1944?

chapter six | FANATICISM AND HATE, MUDDLE AND DELAY

The eventual end of the Third Reich was clear. Two-thirds of the men trapped at Stalingrad had died, and the remaining 90,000 prisoners marched off through the snow to semi-starvation in camps. Some Germans themselves—staff officers of Army Group Centre most obviously—thought of just murdering Hitler (and one or two efforts did get very close to success). But by now the war had created its own momentum, and the mass of Germans were gripped by a surreal paroxysm. Hitler waved aside any mention of peace, and many Germans were executed for defeatism if they doubted *Endsieg*, 'final victory'. How were the western Allies to deal with this? Churchill and Roosevelt met in Casablanca in January 1943 at more or less the same time as Paulus surrendered at Stalingrad, and they now had to plan for cooperation with a victorious Red Army. Stalin himself wanted a second front as soon as possible, an amphibious invasion of France, and was contemptuous of Churchill's prevarications. Eventually the old man, in Moscow in August 1942, had to explode at Stalin, saying why did he think Hitler had not invaded the British Isles after Dunkirk, when there was no army to resist?

The fact was that an amphibious operation over the Channel was just very difficult. In British history, after the Battle of Hastings in 1066, there had only been one successful invasion, that of William of Orange in 1688, and even then that worked only because much of England was on his side. There were not many English invasions of western Europe, either, and some had ended in near-farce, such as the episode at Walcheren against Napoleon in 1809.

Even so, Stalin was right: an invasion should have been possible in 1943, and the Americans—especially George C. Marshall, with his granite-like honesty and his grasp of essentials—knew as much. But at Casablanca, they were not prepared. The British still had the main military hand, they were by now experienced, and with facts and figures could present a case that, given also their superiority in rhetoric, won the Americans over. If Tunis had been taken quickly, perhaps there would still have been time in the campaigning season for a cross-Channel attack. However, there were major delays and Tunis was not cleared until mid-May. A great army, with the wherewithal for an invasion, was thus encamped along the North African shore just south of Italy. The British (or most of them) were in favour of an invasion of Sicily, and the Americans (or most of them) were in favour of something else. But it was the British who won the argument. This shaped the rest of the war.

The fact was that most of the British thought that there must never be a repetition of the Western Front battles, whether of 1916 or of 1940. They had been beaten again and again by the German army, and knew that their own strengths were elsewhere—

the air and the sea. They had done well, better than the Germans, at producing aircraft, and they had a great faith in the efficacy of aerial bombardment—had indeed even set up the world's first strategic instrument for it, Bomber Command. This faith now led, oddly enough, to the equivalent of the Western Front campaigning of 1916, in that failure of an initial effort meant that reinforcement went into the next effort, and after a failure of that, more reinforcement. The air war took a huge amount of the war economy. A bomber contained half a million separate parts, needing precision manufacturing and elaborate maintenance; a third of the British war effort was engaged in aircraft work of one sort or another. Ingenious inventions and adaptations went ahead to make the bombing more effective than in 1941. Surprisingly few voices were raised against the bombing offensive, and in any case it was for a long time the only way in which the British could get back at the Germans, who were anyway blamed for starting it.

By 1945, people in Central Europe looking up into the skies were familiar with the—sometimes—hundreds of silver bombers carrying their incendiaries and high explosives to smash the towns and cities, but the process got going in 1942 and 1943. The Luftwaffe had been designed to help the ground forces, and it had gone into action devastatingly in Poland and then in Holland, bombing cities, particularly Rotterdam, that had been assumed to be defending themselves. It was inevitable that when military targets were attacked, mistakes would be made, and 'collateral damage' came about. It was essentially this that happened with the German bombing, and the RAF struck back;

Hitler did so as well, and the Germans issued a surreal press notice announcing they had dropped more than two million pounds of bombs on London in twenty-four hours. These raids went on until spring 1941. In return the British struck at Mannheim on 16 December 1940, intending this to be an exercise in terror. It was declared to be revenge for the destruction of Southampton in September 1940 and Coventry in November and was ineffective: bombers lost their way, and in any case could not drop bombs with any precision at all. Then in April 1942 they found easier targets. They viciously attacked the picturesque wooden old town of Lübeck, and thereafter this policy was officially 'focused on the morale of the enemy civil population and in particular of the industrial workers'. A 'thousand-bomber raid' was launched against Cologne, the chief Rhineland city, and new tactics were used: 12,000 buildings were damaged or destroyed, though only some 400 people were killed.

In charge of the campaign against the cities was Air Marshal Arthur Harris, who was made commander-in-chief of Bomber Command in 1943. 'Bomber' Harris, as he was called, was utterly single-minded and ruthless. He was convinced that if smashing cities did not win the war outright, it was because they were not being smashed hard enough. He obstinately claimed that he would win the war as the campaign developed, with improvements in accuracy of aim, better crew training, electronic gadgetry to confuse enemy radar, and new tactics—including one by which an initial Pathfinder force dropped incendiary bombs to mark targets for the high explosive of the main force. For attacks in March 1943, the RAF had available 669 heavy bombers and the Americans 300. The US Army Air Forces (USAAF, as the US Air Force was called then) claimed that for much of the war they limited themselves to 'precision' bombing of military targets. But in December 1943, with the introduction of H2X radar sets (which enabled navigation in bad weather), the Americans started bombing cities as well. The British did try industrial targets, and in spring 1943, in the Battle of the Ruhr, dropped 34,000 tons of bombs; after an ingenious raid breaching dams, steel production fell by 200,000 tons. However, Harris did not continue with these raids, which the German armaments minister, Albert Speer, regarded as extremely serious. Instead, the RAF went on with the bombing of cities. Hamburg, in July, was wrecked, because a firestorm developed, as everything combusted after the bombing and charred bodies choked the canals. Two-thirds of the surviving inhabitants had to move house. Of course aircraft production and the output of new tanks were affected, too. Then Harris switched targets to Berlin, meaning to destroy it and end the war by spring 1944. In October 1943 he told the government to be honest with the public about these attacks on civilian targets: no one except for a few high-minded souls would really object if Germans were killed: 'the aim of the Combined Bomber Offensive . . . should be unambiguously stated [as] the destruction of German cities, the killing of German workers, and the disruption of civilized life throughout Germany.' He added, 'It should be emphasized that the destruction of houses, public utilities, transport and lives, the creation of a refugee problem on an unprecedented scale, and the breakdown of morale both at home and at the battle fronts by fear of extended and intensified bombing, are accepted and intended aims of our bombing policy. They are not by-products of attempts to hit factories.' George Orwell satirized this attitude with the imagined headline 'Berlin Bombed: Babies Burn'.

The limited or even counter-productive effects of the bombing offensive were quite soon recognized, however. In the first place, it gave a decisive character to the British war economy, as a very large proportion of the industrial production of the United Kingdom went into heavy bombers, affecting, for instance, output of landing craft. Until 1944, the effect on German production was remarkably small, as it was dispersed. But in that year, coordinated with the RAF, US operations began with Operation Pointblank attacks, designed to hit essential parts of the German economy, such as the ball-bearing works at Schweinfurt, and thus to draw the Luftwaffe into battles that it would lose. Formations of unescorted bombers were very vulnerable, however, and the United States stopped operations until they could produce a long-range fighter. The best of these turned out to be the P-51 Mustang, which was very light (with wood and aluminium) and which therefore had fuel capacity to give it a long range, to Berlin and back to bases in England. The bombing offensive stopped, as such, in April 1944, when the Allies needed to bomb northern France in preparation for the invasion that came in June—much to Harris's dismay. It has been argued that bombing had a limited effect on morale. The postwar British Bombing Survey Unit recognized that the offensive had not worked according to plan: 'The essential premise behind the policy of treating towns as unit targets for area attack, namely that the German economic system was fully extended, was false.' Air losses were vast—the RAF flew nearly 300,000 night sorties and lost 7,500 planes; in 67,000 day sorties, 876. Some 2,800,000 tons of bombs were dropped, nearly half British, with 1944–45 being the worst year. Bombing killed 500,000 Germans overall, and 60,595 British (less than the French figure of 67,078). Over 160,000 Allied airmen were lost in the European theatre.

The claims made for bombing have never been universally accepted or borne out, and in the end there were only two arguments for it. The first was that it greatly distorted the German economy; for the cities to be defended, countless aircraft and guns had to be used over Germany, and were lost to the fighting fronts, especially in Russia. However, the same could have been achieved with a policy of precision bombing of munitions industries and transport systems that kept the military going. The other argument has to do with German morality, not morale. Lionel Bloch, who later became a much-respected legal authority in London, was a young man, in fear for his life, as a Rumanian Jew, in wartime Bucharest. He saw the Germans of the military mission strutting around, full of themselves, as the victories went ahead in 1941, and he remarked that the only way they would ever learn to behave with common sense and humanity was if tons of high explosive were dropped on them, directly. This is unprovable, but the hatred of Germans was so widespread at the time, that such an argument went down well, and supported Harris in everything he undertook, almost to the end, in April 1945, when bombers were quite casually setting out for historic towns on the *Romantische Strasse,* the Romantic Road south of

Würzburg, making a bonfire of them, and sometimes machine-gunning the refugees on the roads. This was the main contribution of the British, but they still in 1943 also had the dominant voice in overall strategy, and that was to mean concentration on the Mediterranean.

Franklin D. Roosevelt, in the circumstances, was under some pressure from his own chiefs of staff to give priority to the Pacific. It was to his credit that the Germany-first policy prevailed, for an enormous wave of anti-Japanese public opinion had built up, and innocent Japanese-American families were being rounded up and deported to camps away from the California coast. Stories came quite quickly of the extraordinarily cruel treatment of captured Americans and Filipinos, and revenge was a very popular call. Besides, there was a considerable likelihood of disaster, as the powerful Japanese navy and air force swept over a vast part of the Pacific, threatening India and Australia. Even though the German war took priority, the Pacific war absorbed enormous resources, specifically of course naval. It required landing craft in particular, which were in any case in short supply: the British had concentrated on building bombers, and the Americans on building ships, in order to make up for any shortfall that the U-boats might cause. They also put a huge effort into aircraft carriers, and as soon as Pearl Harbor happened, they commissioned thirteen of them—leading in the end to crushing superiority—as well as submarines. This sheer weight gave the navy priority in repelling and then pushing back the Japanese. The army had had a great blow when the Philippines fell, but the Americans could read most Japanese codes, and when the Japanese navy reached the Coral Sea, 500 miles to the northeast, they were ready. Fought in early May 1942, the Battle of the Coral Sea was the first major naval battle between ships that did not even sight each other, and the first in which aircraft carriers engaged each other. Each side lost a carrier, and the Japanese withdrew.

Then came the decisive battle, Midway, in June. The Japanese naval chief, Isoroku Yamamoto, knew the United States and well understood that a giant was mobilizing against him. He would get a blow in, and try to destroy the remaining carriers. A large force was therefore sent to draw the Americans to battle in the very centre of the Pacific Ocean. The Japanese made a diversionary attack on the Aleutian Islands, but their main assault was at Wake Island, and especially the Midway Atoll. But as the Americans could read Japanese codes, they moved their fleet out of harm's way without being detected. The Japanese mustered an enormous force, and heavily bombed the US aircraft base at Midway, though not decisively, on 4 June. There were several American responses that failed and therefore gave the Japanese an idea that they were safe: ground-based bombers missed their targets, and then carrier-based aircraft with torpedoes, which needed a long and flat run at their targets, were smashed by Japanese Zero fighters. The Japanese admiral then wondered whether to attack Midway again, or to search out and hit the American warships. He decided first the one, then the other, and his aircraft were being armed on the decks, with fuel and ammunition at hand, when another American force struck, this time dive bombers. Four Japanese aircraft carriers were sunk. It was the most rapid, decisive battle in history—within five minutes, the Japanese had lost their large superiority and were at equal numbers in carriers. Yamamoto had another huge force still in reserve, and expected the Americans to follow up their victory, but they did not. Now this war would be fought in two different sectors, MacArthur with the army on the Australian side—New Guinea was larger than France and took a good year to subdue— and Admiral Chester Nimitz with the navy in the central Pacific, with many tough islands to crack.

The next major fight would be at the island of Guadalcanal, in the Solomon Islands, east of New Guinea, where the Japanese were building a big air base. In August 1942, some 16,000 Marines landed, but over the next six months the Japanese fed in troops and aircraft, the supply convoys themselves having battles at sea: losses were immense on both sides, but the Japanese could not afford them, whereas the Americans could. In February 1943, they won, and in June began island hopping forward, in order to isolate the Japanese base at Rabaul. This was all done with bravura, but the Japanese resistance was spectacular, and it was going to be a long, long way to Tokyo. There was going to be a similar long haul for the British Indian army. It had pulled out of Burma when the Japanese attacked in 1942—a terrible, gruelling march across soaking jungle to the borders of India. The British Indian army had not really been prepared for a world war: the main purpose had been domestic security, and the Indian Nationalists, trying to exploit British embarrassments, were eager to get the British to 'Quit India' as their slogan ran. In fact the British managed to restore order quite easily and the Indian army remained loyal as it expanded and served in various theatres, including the Middle East. However, the initial disasters in Burma had a knock-on effect in Bengal, the shipping and rice imports of which were badly disrupted; and Churchill gave priority to the war effort, neglecting civilian needs. The result was a severe famine, in which three million people starved to death. The Burmese theatre mattered because it provided a land route to China, where American forces cooperated with Chiang Kai-shek's Nationalists as the Japanese tried to extend their control of this vast country. In 1943, the British pushed across the Burmese border, not to much effect, and subsequently the Japanese tried themselves to invade India in the spring of 1944. It was their turn to encounter difficulties of supply, and of 85,000 men, 55,000 were casualties, 30,000 of them dead, often because of starvation. The British were able, with Chinese assistance, to open the way to Chiang's capital at Chungking (Chongqing)—although as it happened the Japanese launched an offensive in 1944, which greatly damaged the Nationalist army. The decisive events in the Asian war had to come from the American island-hopping campaign.

All these fronts were grindingly difficult. The Japanese were grimly holding on everywhere though they had no real idea how they might plausibly win the war. There were any number of Pacific islands to be taken, bases attacked from the air and isolated. To reach the Philippines, the Mariana Islands would have to be occupied; to reach them, the Marshalls; to reach them, tiny atolls northeast of Guadalcanal beyond the Coral Sea. But the islands were very difficult targets. One such, Tarawa, was assaulted in

November 1943, and of the 4,500 defenders, hardly one survived. In June 1944 Saipan, to the east of the Philippines, was defended by 30,000 men, sheltered in caves, almost none of whom survived, and their women and children jumped over cliffs to avoid capture. The Japanese were now having enormous difficulty in supplying their maritime empire, because submarines sank 1,300 of their merchantmen (of which 124 carried tanks and 320 troops), which were anyway, by an astonishing misjudgement, hardly convoyed. This made little difference to the fanaticism of Japanese resistance. In June 1944 the Americans entered the first approaches to Japan herself, the Marianas, with fifteen carriers, nearly a thousand planes, and an armada of warships. The Japanese planes were becoming obsolete, knocked out in what became known as the Great Marianas Turkey Shoot, victims of the new American radar and anti-aircraft shells. Most of the Japanese submarines were destroyed; for a combat loss of some thirty American planes (though another 100 fell victim to crash landings and fuel shortage), the Japanese lost 450, almost all with their crews, and three irreplaceable carriers. It was the end of the Japanese carrier force, and towards the close of 1944, MacArthur returned, as promised, to the Philippines and the Americans' two arms were closing in on the home islands.

German resistance from 1943 had a similar quality of fanaticism to that of the Japanese. That the war would end in catastrophic defeat was now clear, but Hitler's assumption was that he would be saved in the end by some piece of luck—citing doubtful historical precedent, such as the fortuitous death of the Russian Empress Elizabeth in 1762, which saved Prussia from collapse in the Seven Years War because her successor was a fanatical admirer of the Prussian army. Hitler was set to go on to the bitter end, counting on new armaments such as the jet engine or the Schnorkel submarine; work on nuclear fission was also going ahead, though it had no priority, and there were rumours of a death ray. If this had been an old-fashioned war, he would have contacted the Russians for a reversal of alliances, but though there were men in the German Foreign Office who surreptitiously approached the Soviet representative in Stockholm, they had no backup support. When they approached the British, they also got nowhere, and when some attempted to blow up Hitler in July 1944, the names of Germans who had tried to talk to the British were revealed on the BBC, a decision shaped by panic that Stalin would otherwise think that the British were trying to deal with Hitler behind his back. They were executed, and their families interned in camps. The German paroxysm thereby increased, its surreal side becoming accentuated. When some sensible senior officers who had been captured at Stalingrad appealed for a German military league that would raise an army against Hitler, they also had very little response; and at the end, when villagers in Baden were liberated by the Americans, some of them went up the hill to where the Gestapo were hiding, and solemnly denounced their neighbours for defeatism. This was going to be a war, both with Germany and Japan, that would go on to a very bitter end. Still, it was not yet being fought where it would in the end have to be fought, in France. The upshot of the diversions and the side shows was that the main Anglo-American effort was now being made in the Mediterranean, against the least of the Axis Powers, Italy.

It was obvious that Italy could now be knocked out of the war. Its military was in ruins. The Allies invaded Sicily on 9 July 1943, but it was no exemplary performance: they played it safe, plodding round the island's perimeter and just pushing the Germans over the narrow strait to the toe of Italy. In late July a coup deposed Mussolini, and the king, Victor Emmanuel III, had him arrested by troops loyal to the Crown. Mussolini was spirited away, eventually to a mountain resort in the Apeninnes, from where Hitler rescued him by air; he was installed as ruler of a Fascist Republic based in the north, under German protection, at the little town of Salò on Lake Garda, but it was a sinister-operetta state. Italy changed sides on September 8, but there was considerable muddle as regards the terms of surrender and yet more muddle as regards the invasion of the mainland. In the event the landing at the toe (3 September, as the armistice was signed) was pointless as the British Eighth Army marched 300 miles north to the Salerno area against no opposition. Plans for airborne landings also came to nothing; the only real success happened when Taranto, at the heel, fell, but again there was delay and muddle in exploiting this success. Of course the Germans should now have been contemplating a coup against Hitler similar to that against Mussolini, but that did not happen: Nazism had been far more ruthless in eliminating opposition than Fascism in Italy, where monarchy, church, and army were all centres of potential resistance. In mid-August, the Germans had activated an army group under Rommel, with a new army in southern Italy, under the formidable Albert Kesselring. The Germans were fortunate that the nature of the land in the toe of

Italy made it very difficult for the Allies to bypass obstacles and the Germans efficiently destroyed the region's bridges. They concentrated, therefore, elsewhere. The Americans had expected that the Italian surrender would make the landing at Salerno a formality, but when they landed they ran into scraped-together German battle groups. German reinforcements arrived, counterattacked, and were really only stopped by colossal bombardment from air and sea, with over a thousand tons of bombs dropped daily. The Allies finally gained Salerno on 18 September and Foggia airport, an important one for attack on southern Germany and the Balkans, nine days later. By early October, the whole of southern Italy was in the Allies' hands, but they faced a set of formidable defensive lines on which Kesselring could stage exhausting resistance. The Germans had flooded the Pontine Marshes and diverted rivers as well, to swamp valleys. The American Fifth Army took six weeks to struggle seven miles to the main German Gustav Line, where the great fortress-like Benedictine abbey of Monte Cassino dominated the landscape with the classic thick and ancient walls of such monasteries. The Germans, appreciating its historic status, promised not to use it for military purposes, but the Americans suspected that it helped observation of their lines, and they attacked it four times. Having failed to take it, they then flattened it, though that solved nothing, because the Germans now had better cover, in the rubble, and the weather was foul enough to defeat all efforts from 17 January to 18 May. Finally, twenty Allied divisions on a twenty-mile-long front dislodged the Germans, mainly because French Algerians and Moroccans had worked their way round the hills behind the front.

Churchill wanted to speed up the Italian operation. He hoped to use naval and air superiority for another amphibious assault, this time at Anzio, south of Rome. It was his last independent strategic initiative. The whole scheme made sense only in terms of energy and surprise. But the Chiefs of Staff wanted landing craft to be shifted elsewhere in February, and so the Anzio landing came at the wrong time, late in January, when troops were still tired. It began well, and a patrolling jeep even reached Rome, but the American general, John Lucas, was desperately prudent, anxious to consolidate his base, and German troops responded with energy (and were assisted by a plague of mosquitoes from the flooded Pontine). They ceaselessly bombed the landing beachheads, and the Allies could not break out until late in May, by which time the Cassino line had already been breached. On top of everything else, vanity got in the way of proper victory. Instead of striking inland to cut the German retreat from Cassino, the American Mark Clark, already overshadowed by Dwight Eisenhower and George Patton, decided his name should be in lights as the taker of Rome, and he even arrested British officers who broke his ban on their also entering the city. The Germans managed to get away far to the east, undisturbed, with seven divisions, and the Allies' capture of Rome came absurdly late, overshadowed by Normandy. There was this to be said for Anzio, that following the landings, the German High Command dropped plans to transfer five of Kesselring's best divisions to northwest Europe, which gave obvious help as regards the invasion of France. But the cost to the Allies was high—up to the fall of Rome, 43,000 casualties, while the German army in southern and central Italy survived intact for another year. All in all, given the tremendous reversals that Germany had suffered at the end of 1942, this was an extraordinary turn of events. But in 1944, the fate of Sodom and Gomorrah was to be rained down on Central Europe. The end might have occurred a year earlier had the diversions of strength into Italy and the illusions of Bomber Command been less thick.

WORLD WAR TWO

chapter seven | NAZISM AND COMMUNISM

preceding page: Jews being rounded up in the Warsaw Ghetto, some time in 1943 (Corbis)

As the 'Anglo-Americans' and the 'Asiatic hordes' closed in, Germany was under siege. More and more, the Nazis claimed that they were fighting for 'The New Europe'. This was the name of a magazine published by Josef Goebbels, the minister for propaganda, and its title as well as its articles have a familiar ring: 'Europe is fighting for unity', 'Youth ensures Europe's future', and 'The economic unity of Europe'; another title, though, is less anodyne: 'The New Europe: a victory over Anglo-Saxon hostility'. Especially after 1942, as the bombs devastated Germany's cities and the armies retreated in the east, such talk went ahead, and highly placed Frenchmen sometimes joined in (their souls, and on occasion their bodies, went marching on in the Europe that was to emerge in the 1950's).

Under the shock of defeat, the French government that had taken over, with its little capital at Vichy, set about a programme of national regeneration. Some of its ministers were industrial technicians, anxious to make France great again in collaboration with a Germany that they admired for its ruthlessness and efficiency. They had to flee when the Allies invaded, ending up at Sigmaringen castle in southwestern Germany: tubby, be-suited figures quarrelling as to who had the room with the view (an episode memorably recalled by the novelist Louis-Ferdinand Céline, a black-humour virtuoso who was Marshal Pétain's doctor). In 1943, they would discuss, with their German masters, how to match the French and German economies. It is astonishing what a mess they made of it. The resources of occupied and satellite Europe ought to have given Hitler a war economy to match that of the Americans and British. As things were, France, from 1940 to 1944, produced only 2,500 aircraft, mostly trainers. The only places to produce more in wartime than before were Belgium and the Czech lands, which were, relatively speaking, pampered (and also, to be fair, untouched by bombing).

German occupation authorities exploited any economy they could control, with an exchange rate absurdly in their favour. They bought up dirt-cheap what they could—in the case of Goering, paintings from the blackmailed Parisian Jewish art dealers. In Paris, people got about by makeshift bicycle and lost a third of their weight, though in part this was because of the hate-filled relationship between town and peasant. In Holland in the winter of 1944–45 there was real starvation, people reduced to eating tulip bulbs, but food supplies were kept up in Vienna to the very end of the war, even with the Russians in the suburbs at Mödling, and Slovakia, with its peasant agriculture and lack of large towns, remained piled with food. But using western European economic strength in any logical way was beyond the German authorities, some of whom were anyway brutal, stupid figures. French industry needed German coal and machinery if it was to get going, and the chief planner on the German side, Albert Speer, did indeed sympathize, meeting his counterpart, Jean Bichelonne on friendly terms. But while machinery went west, Fritz Sauckel, in charge of wartime labour, was forcing hundreds of thousands of French workmen to the east, and the whole business was bedevilled by the miserable wages and conditions that prevailed for foreign labourers in Germany (some industrialists involved were later charged with war crimes). It was true that, as the bombing sharpened men's minds, munitions output was rationalized in the sense that unskilled Ukrainian women were employed on a moving factory belt, there to repeat the same mechanical exercise on a single part, until at the other end an aircraft or a gun emerged. Before then, teams of skilled workmen had competed to complete single aircraft, and to a very high standard of finish; German workmen were of course known for their devotion, and to the very end of the war, apprenticeships were still formally taking four years as each apprentice had to master four separate sets of skills. But such exactitude put a severe limit on output. There were huge mis-investments—three vast Austrian aero-engine works were started in 1938 but so inefficiently managed that they only began producing in 1943, whereupon they were bombed to bits. Germany produced hardly more war goods than Great Britain alone, and for some of the time many fewer aircraft. Speer did step up output, but this was very much at the expense of reliability. In 1944, for example, the naval yards at last produced a prototype submarine that could stay submerged for very prolonged periods, charging its batteries unobserved, but its first showing to the public, at Danzig, ended in farce: the welding had been botched, and it was sinking; it had to be towed at night back to the dock. Aircraft were produced in 1944 of course, but the shortfall of experienced pilots was such that they were speedily shot down: in the last year of the war, almost all pilots who emerged, green, from the training schools were knocked out after a month. In the circumstances, 1943 was the last year in which Germany's strengths could still be matched to the needs of the moment: heavy tanks appeared, though not in adequate numbers.

But if the Nazis could not make of occupied Europe what they might have done, there was one matter where a sinister efficiency did appear. In mid-September 1941, as Kiev was being taken, with more than half a million Soviet prisoners of war, Hitler thought he had won the war. In Rastenburg, the mood was of jubilation, and Heinrich Himmler visited. Himmler was head of the SS, the Nazi Party élite element, and also chief of police, director of the security services in the occupied areas, and master of a concentration-camp empire. A Gestapo department, headed by Adolf Eichmann, dealt with Jewish matters, and though discussion of these was supposed to be secret, we can deduce that, that September, Himmler and Hitler came up with a plan for the total elimination of the Jews from Europe. Hitler had after all said, in a speech of January 1939, that he would eliminate them if he was provoked, though at the time the main idea was to expel them from Germany, or at any rate from public life (just over half of German Jews did in fact manage to leave their country). But in occupied eastern Europe, the Nazis were much more forthright. They made out that Jews and Communists were the same thing, and Hitler decreed before moving on the Soviet Union that both should just be executed out of hand. Already in Poland, the three million Jews had been herded into ghettos, a few very overcrowded and insanitary streets, in which disease spread. Special organizations in the army's rear—*Einsatzkommandos*—went around butchering Jews, lining them up along ditches and shooting them so that they fell into mass graves. Local populations sometimes helped for they hated Communists and sometimes identified them with Jews. Himmler had come to say—we can suppose—that this was all very messy and needed to be rationalized. From that moment on, the Jews of Germany and of all occupied Europe were under a deadly threat. There were bureaucratic obstacles, and some people with a conscience used these to delay the inevitable: what to do about Jewish property, how to define a Jew, what to do with foreign-passport Jews, and so forth. To sort these matters out, a conference was held in a villa in the Berlin suburb of Wannsee in January 1942, and it entered history, not strictly accurately, as the moment when the decision was taken to exterminate the Jews. It cleared away the legal obstacles, and the catastrophe went ahead. The Jews of Russia and Poland were in any event being butchered or killed in other ways, by starvation and disease. The programme now extended to western Europe, and Jews there were to be transported to camps in Poland. Until the outbreak of war, the emphasis had been on pushing the Jews out, on the grounds that they were a bad influence—yellow press, modern art, Communism, etc. Those who remained faced endless humiliations both petty and major, such as the prohibition on birdseed for pet birds or on parcels from abroad, but they could not exactly be murdered. Goebbels, as *Gauleiter,* or Nazi Party leader, of Berlin, mercilessly harassed the Jews remaining in the city. Now, after Wannsee, the way was clear for Europe's Jews to be exterminated.

And so began the Holocaust. Jews were to be registered, and deported by train to the east—Riga, Minsk, various places in Poland. There, those who were physically capable of labour would work, and those who were incapable would receive *Sonderbehandlung,* 'special treatment', as it was known. Eventually, gas chambers were used, and the most famous of these were in the vast camp of Auschwitz, on the old German-Polish border. The first deportees arrived from Germany in December 1941, and were shot. From spring 1942, the Polish ghettos were emptied and were almost vacant by summer 1943, when there came at last a revolt by those who were left (they had acquired some pistols from the Polish resistance). A few survivors managed to hide beyond the ghetto walls. Roman Polanski's film *The Pianist* is a brilliant evocation of those times. The Jews of France and Italy, though subjected to vicious laws, mainly survived because religious institutions, private persons, and some people in authority connived to prevent deportation (Huguenot mayors in France dished out false papers); Belgian Jews were tacitly protected by the German military governor, Alexander von Falkenhausen, who was tried but pardoned after the war. The Belgian Jews, like the French, had enough freedom of manoeuvre to be cunning, or perhaps it was just that in Belgium or France people were accustomed to dealing with an oppressive and inquisitive state. When told to set up a Jewish council, they found ways of not doing so. In Holland where the state counted, north European fashion, as honest and decent, they did set up such a council, and once the bureaucracy was in place it had tamely to hand over names and addresses that it kept on lists of charity appeals. These Jews were picked up and gradually sent to the death camps, by Dutch police—about ninety percent of Dutch Jews, in a country where anti-Semitism was so limited that there was even a general strike in protest against their fate. In January 1945 the Jewish council staged a small party, to congratulate themselves on keeping the community together (they too were deported, but to Theresienstadt near Prague, the supposedly privileged camp that was used as a showcase for Red Cross inspectors and the like: when they returned to Holland, they were tried for collaboration). The Vatican behaved carefully, and came in for much criticism for not doing enough to protect Jews, but Hitler said at least once that when the war was over his next enemy would be the Catholic Church, and he could have wiped out the Pope's neutral status at a nod. In Catholic Slovakia and Croatia, the Vatican protested energetically and managed to halt deportations; the Pope and influential neutrals also interfered in the horrors in Hungary when they got going in 1944.

The conventional figure for Jews killed is six million, though how many were gassed and how many were starved or overworked to death is impossible to determine. Auschwitz itself was not just a death camp: it housed a sub-camp, Monowitz, with a chemical plant (still in use in today's Poland) where efforts were made, under the IG Farben combine, to produce synthetic rubber (they failed). Specialist Jewish workers might survive there, as valuable, though in general they died of demoralization or as a result of brutality. In notorious cases, ambitious doctors used camp inmates for experimentation—how much cold or starvation a body could stand, for instance, or how twins responded to this or that treatment. The most famous, Dr Josef Mengele, was the ambitious sprig of a small-town Catholic family in Baden (it made agricultural machinery) and had studied medicine, of which the then most progressive element counted as genetics. He got himself, through his supervisor in Frankfurt, to Auschwitz after a spell on the Eastern Front, and prided himself on stopping an epidemic of typhus (he used gas to kill the infectious sick, and had the remains cremated in the famous installations). Then he got busy with genetic experiments, and had his grisly box of findings ready for his professor when the camp was evacuated. He was hurt that he was not recognised, and resisted his family's orders to run away at once (eventually he fled to Buenos Aires where for a time he had a chemist's shop marked 'Mengele'). Very senior doctors were involved in all of this, and Mengele's professor, Baron Otmar von Verschuer, rose high after the war in West Germany. Churchill had it absolutely right when he warned the world that if the Nazis won, there would be a great darkness of perverted science. Orwell made the same point when he said that the Hitlerian vision of the future was just of 250,000,000 blond people reproducing themselves.

The question was often asked after the war as to how much ordinary Germans had known of what went on. When the British bombing got under way, ordinary Germans called it retribution for what had been done to the Jews. There were rumours of hideous atrocities in the east, rumours that were repeated by German generals in British captivity (they were sometimes but by no means always shocked). The details of the Final Solution were not known, were kept secret as far as possible, with camouflage words such as *Sonderbehandlung*. Much of the programme depended upon collaboration, in some cases even of Jewish councils. For instance, in Holland there were six SS officers engaged, and in Auschwitz itself, to which a million people were sent, the camp guards did not number more than 3,000, even then mainly non-German. If the SS ran into proper obstruction or resistance, it was seriously hampered, as was the case in France or Italy, where even anti-Semites were moved to protect the Jews from the worst horrors; in the siege of Budapest early in 1945, German officers themselves deliberately ignored the existence of a Jewish refuge run by a Lutheran pastor just under one of their bulwarks in the castle district. But the whole idea of exterminating Europe's Jews was unimaginable, and many people, including Jews, simply did not believe the story when it was revealed, via a shocked German industrialist, to the Jewish Committee in neutral Switzerland on 1 August 1942. News came out in dribs and drabs, but it was only in 1944 that the facts became plain, as the Russians uncovered the evidence of the camps that the Germans had tried to destroy, and Auschwitz itself was freed only in January 1945, by which time columns of skeletal inmates were being whipped along the snowy roads to different camps in Germany.

Hitler's central belief was in the superiority of the Aryan, a belief that went back to the German Romantics' worship of ancient Greece. This superiority could be turned into the 'Triumph of the Will', meaning that Aryan intelligence and drive could, with Aryan will power, succeed in anything. Leni Riefenstahl (with a Jewish grandparent) made a film dedicated to this theme, *Triumph of the Will,* documenting the 1934 Nazi Party Congress in Nuremberg. Another film, *Olympia*, with a prelude of sexless loinclothed perfect bodies, documented the most famous Olympics of all time, in 1936 in Berlin (during which the African-American athlete Jesse Owens embodied a devastating critique of Nazi notions of white race superiority). Hitler's own career had exemplified this triumph of the will, and he was sure that German science would produce miracle weapons that would in the end defeat the corrupt west and the swarming east. Right to the very end, when the Russians had seized the Prussian ministry of finance, Germans went on believing that, somehow, a monstrous death-ray would be produced, to annihilate their enemies, and in Prague, in April 1945, officials were still going round schools measuring children's feet to judge whether they qualified racially as Germans. What is so extraordinary about it all is that Hitler himself said, in February 1945, that it had been a wasted effort, that it was impossible to work out what race really involved. But he had indoctrinated the nation, especially the young, many of whom, in uniform, were fanatical in their hatred and contempt for non-Germans—Slavs and Jews particularly.

The surrender at Stalingrad had been a tremendous blow to Hitler's prestige. Now he was threatened on all fronts—the air, at sea, in the west, in the south—while his allies dropped away or, in the case of Japan, were undergoing controlled demolition. The recovery at Kharkov had given him, nonetheless, some respite, and he intended to use that to retake the initiative in Russia. With new weapons in his arsenal, he ordered an offensive, called Citadel, centring on Kursk and Oryol. Citadel was based in part on faulty intelligence: that the Russians were not capable of much. But though their total losses had been enormous, over 12,000,000 men to date, they proved still to have 5,700,000 in the field to the Germans' 2,700,000. They had lost, it was thought, 21,000 tanks. Though the Germans had also lost a huge amount, their production, and in quality as much as quantity, was recovering. In 1943 they turned out 6,000 tanks, two-fifths of them heavy Tigers or medium Panthers, which, when they appeared, so frightened some Russian tank crews that they jumped out of their machines and ran. Now the German High Command could see that Stalin might assault the great bend of the Dniepr, thinly held, vulnerable from south and north, and vital to the German war economy—the coal of Stalino (aka Donetsk), the hydro-electricity of Zaporozhye (open again in January 1943), and the manganese of Nikopol. Paul Pleiger, in charge of the Nazis' coal supplies, even said that without the six or seven million tons of Donbass coal they could not increase arms production. The original plan for Citadel was not senseless. Hitler went back and forth to the advanced headquarters at Zaporozhye, arguing against Manstein's preferred plans for a mobile defensive, simply on the grounds that certain terrain could not be abandoned. Still, transfer of the troops took much longer than expected because of air attacks, partisan assaults, destruction of bridges, and even the sheer difficulty of turning a train to face in the opposite direction. The attack might have made sense in April, but was endlessly postponed, and the Russians knew very well from many sources what was going to happen. The British, reading German messages, knew. They knew also that Stalin would not trust them. And so they used again, as before Barbarossa, their dummy spy ring, 'Lucy', in Switzerland, which was supposed to be getting information from a German staff officer, which they passed off as a Communist espionage arrangement to let Stalin know directly. And Stalin knew in turn from his British spy—John Cairncross, who held high office in the governments of 1940–41—what elaborate deceptions were going on. But the German plan was obvious. The line jutted far to the west, with the town of Kursk at its head, but the Germans also stood in salients north—Oryol—and south—Belgorod—from which they could famously operate pincers.

The Battle of Kursk began on 5 July. It counts as the greatest land battle in history—three million soldiers, 69,000 guns, 13,000 tanks, and 12,000 aircraft. The offensive itself was misconceived—a frontal attack without surprise, and this was quite contrary to the lessons of 1940. Guderian had really developed the Panzer attack from the earlier 1918 shock troops, going along lines of least resistance. But now, the place and even the time of the attack were known, and defensive preparations had been made well in advance—on the Voronezh front alone there were 2,600 miles of trenches, with nearly a million mines, in the essential parts of the front. The Germans were even quite weak in tanks, despite legend, with only 328 ultra-modern ones (out of 2,500). The battle began on 5 July at 3:30 in the morning. The Red Air Force started the action, though the Luftwaffe was able to knock out most of the 400 bombers launched. General Walter Model with the northern pincer used only a few of his tanks, probably wanting to spare them for the Soviet offensive he knew was coming. Some Ferdinands, weighing seventy tons and supposedly invulnerable, were stuck in a Russian trench system and half of the Tigers were wrecked by mines. On the 13th Model's attack had to be stopped altogether so that one of those vast Russian attacks, which a Panzer army staff member compared to a landslide, could be held off. On the southern side Manstein used all his tanks including the 100 Tigers and 200 Panthers, which did indeed turn out to be greatly superior to Russian tanks but testing on them had not been complete, and a quarter dropped out even before action, and some caught fire from defective pump systems. Twenty-five were victims of an un-cleared minefield, the sappers having to work under artillery fire. The attack on the right, towards Prokhorovka, went faster, for the Russians panicked before the Tigers and Panthers, which were invulnerable frontally and could knock out a T-34 tank from 6,500 feet with a high-velocity gun. On 6 July, Nikolai Fyodor-ovich Vatutin of the Voronezh Army Group was given the strate-gic reserve; he was supposed to start the counter-offensive and had 2,924 tanks (by 20 July) but ordered most of them dug in.

Even, on 8 July, when a mass Soviet tank attack on a logistical centre occurred, a single Tiger, under repair but usable, took on fifty tanks, knocking out twenty-two T-34s, while the others fled. Prokhorovka became famous as the scene of an immense tank clash on 12 July, but this was a clever confection thought up by a Soviet general to obscure his own misdeeds—the Germans here lost only three dozen tanks, whereas the Red Army very clumsily threw in about a thousand and let them be fired on from the vulnerable side in a German ambush when they fell into an anti-tank ditch that had been forgotten about. The facts as to this were not revealed until 1990, almost fifty years later. In fact Hitler called off Kursk partly because the aircraft were diverted to the south and more particularly because the Allies had landed in Sicily on 10 July. Manstein protested that he should go on, that the Russians had lost 1,800 tanks, that he had not used his reserve, and he did indeed prepare a lesser operation but Hitler halted it on the 16th. Russian losses at Kursk were enormous—319,000 men (to 55,000), 2,000 tanks (250), and 2,000 aircraft (159), but, as Manstein said, the Red Army was a hydra, two heads grew for every one that was lopped off. Counter-offensives followed hard on Kursk. Model's army on the Oryol side was hit from 12 July to 18 August, then Manstein's at Belgorod on the southern side, from 3 to 13 August, and there were attacks to relieve Leningrad from the east (the river Volkhov) and Tver (Kalinin) where the Germans still threatened Moscow. By now Manstein's commanders had 240 tanks, and the 800 planes of the Fourth Air Corps had to cover the whole of the southern front as it bulged far to the east, and the entire Eastern

Front was in flames. Kharkov once more and for good was lost on 23 August—much of it in ruins. Again the Russians suffered enormous casualties—eight to one, and the Red Army was disappointed as Stalin had hoped to reach East Prussia by the end of 1943 and had failed.

After Kursk, the Germans were simply on the retreat. They were unable except briefly, here and there, to take the initiative. Besides, they plodded, without petrol, by horse and cart, whereas the Russians now moved in American vehicles and with American tinned supplies: they were mobile even in deep winter. Hitler had to divert strength to the Mediterranean theatres, and would do so again to France, such that the eastern armies were open to Russian attack. Besides, the overall line was extraordinarily difficult. After Kursk, it ran roughly along the river Dniepr to the east, and Manstein's headquarters were at Zaporozhye, at the extreme eastern point of the bend. The front then extended east again, to the river Mius, which connected with the Donets and the Sea of Azov, protecting the Crimea, and Army Group A had only narrowly managed to escape via the Kerch Peninsula and Rostov. Manstein would have preferred a retreat and then counter-attack, but Hitler wanted to keep the Donbass minerals, so tensions arose. The other army groups were better concentrated, but the problem was much the same—weakness of force, scantiness of communications, vulnerability of transport.

The German forces on the Caucasus edge were by August too weak to repulse a Soviet attack. They had to fall back all the way through the Donbass to the Dniepr, so losing anyway the industrial resources and half the farmland that Germany had invaded the Soviet Union to exploit. As October began, the Germans found the Dniepr line impossible to hold as the Soviet bridgeheads grew, and important towns started to fall, with Zaporozhye the first to go, followed by Dniepropetrovsk. Finally, early in November the Soviets broke out of their bridgeheads on either side of Kiev and captured it. The Soviet advance continued along the railway line until the 1939 Polish-Soviet border was reached on 3 January 1944. The Germans assumed that the thick snow and then the mud would hold up the Red Army, but this time the Russians just kept coming and coming. German divisions avoided utter disaster only by a thin margin, and the 1943–44 campaigning season had brought the Russians five hundred miles forward. In 1944, the Red Army took back Odessa on 10 April and then Sevastopol over a month later. The loss of Bryansk, and more importantly Smolensk, on 25 September cost the Germans the keystone of their entire defensive system. In January the following year, with utter surprise, the Volkhov and Baltic army groups struck at Leningrad, and pushed the Germans back to Novgorod and the Estonian border. The way was now open for the German collapse.

WORLD WAR TWO

chapter eight | WEST AND EAST

preceding page: American troops en route to Normandy, June 1944 (Bettmann/Corbis)

As the Germans pulled back from the Caucasus, the oil no longer under threat of takeover, whether there or in Iran, Stalin became of much greater account. Russia in a way had returned to the position she had had before the Crimean War. She was again a great power with a menacing ideology. This was all Hitler's doing: the enormous crisis of 1941 and 1942 had acted as such a shock to the system that the Soviet leadership was forced to rationalize at last—to stop mismanaging the economy and to promote the right men in the right way to run the armed forces. At any rate, Moscow was back. As a sign of that, Stalin deigned to travel from Moscow, though, as a precaution, only as far as Teheran, in an Iran that was occupied by the British and Russians. The decisive inter-allied conference took place there, in November 1943, as the Red Army was retaking Kiev and closing in on the old border. At Teheran, Russian domination of eastern Europe was implicitly recognized, and this was done as a bargain over Churchill's head. At one point, he even stormed out of a dinner, in protest at a remark of Stalin's about the murderous things he meant to do in Germany. It had been, Stalin explained, a joke.

The link between Churchill and Roosevelt was growing weaker. The two needed, for the sake of war-time popular opinion, to make a show of getting on well; both men were actors, and there was of course some mutual understanding between two aristocrats of the Atlantic world. Churchill's act was tremendous, and even when people were very irritated by him, he could disarm them. In spring 1944, contemplating the run-down of British power, he became depressed, holding his head in his hands. His wife, Clementine, said, 'Cheer up, just think how Mussolini is feeling now.' Churchill answered: 'At least he got to shoot his son-in-law' (Mussolini having put Galeazzo Ciano on trial for treason at Verona in January). Roosevelt could put on a fireworks display of charm, while all the time calculating what was to be his next move. Tensions came up between the two men. Now that the war was being won, were the British (and the French) to restore their empires? Roosevelt and almost all Americans did not approve of empires, and would certainly not pay to sustain them: there was endless haggling over the terms of Lend-Lease so as to stop the British from using the help to promote their own exports (Churchill protested: Empires don't haggle; his opposite number said: Republics do). In July 1944, at an important meeting at Bretton Woods in New Hampshire to organize the finances and trade of the postwar world, the British fielded their star, John Maynard Keynes. Even he, with rhetorical powers that had the entire conference giving him a standing ovation when, exhausted, he had to leave, could not persuade the Americans to be generous with the purse strings. It was only in 1947 that the British learned how to deal with these problems: if the Americans threatened them with collapse, then they would indeed collapse. At the turn of 1943–44, the American military weight in Europe was almost as great as the British, and would soon be greater; and there were serious rifts over strategy. The Americans wanted to get the war over with as fast as possible, and were prepared for a huge invasion of France, whereas many of the British feared disaster, and this view was far from senseless. There had been only three successful amphibious operations so far—the Dunkirk evacuation, which had been in the wrong direction; Torch, which had succeeded against feeble opposition; and Madagascar in May 1942 to stop the Vichy colonial government from assisting the Japanese. The Red Army just at the moment of Teheran was having a bad experience with amphibious landings in the Crimea, where tanks were landed too far out, artillery and infantry did not cooperate, and the air force was ineffective. The British preferred to go on with the bombing campaign and were ambitious as regards the Mediterranean. The Anglo-American conferences had become tense, and matters were not helped by the disdainful attitudes of Montgomery (as Churchill said of him, 'In defeat, indomitable; in advance, invincible; in victory, insufferable').

Churchill kept trying to find an alternative to the amphibious invasion, and had been persuaded of the Mediterranean. But Italy is a country to invade from the north; now, from the south, in a wet and cold autumn, the Allies encountered the Gothic Line, a ten-mile-deep set of fortifications along the Apennines with the usual concrete firing posts, anti-tank ditches, minefields, and hundreds of thousands of yards of barbed wire. Churchill (and the American commanders on the spot) spoke, with some weight, that the Italian campaign should be seen through, but it did involve an endless plod by over a million men, and a commitment of bombing aircraft (sometimes with devastating effects on Italy's monuments). Maybe, thought Churchill, the whole business could be made easier if extended to the Balkans. There was a German army group in Greece, and another in Yugoslavia. If the Turks entered the war, they could, together with the British, cut off these forces. On the map this looked plausible, and Churchill saw the Turkish leader, İsmet İnönü, after leaving Teheran. Oddly enough, a later and much more imaginative Turkish leader, Turgut Özal, said that İnönü's greatest mistake was not to join in: he could have struck a grand bargain with the British and the Greeks, and taken the Aegean islands from Italy. But İnönü's vice was paralyzing prudence, and maybe in the end he was right: if Turkey's intervention had gone wrong, she would have been 'saved' by the Soviet Union and lost land and sovereignty, even over Istanbul. To show what he could do, Churchill encouraged an occupation of the large and picturesque islands off the Turkish coast with Rhodes the main prize. It was a fiasco, the Italian surrender mishandled, command of the air not secured, amphibious operations gone wrong, and Rhodes never reached. The Germans re-occupied Kos and Leros, two of the larger islands, and captured thousands of British soldiers—their last significant victory which, horribly, they used to round up local Jews of Rhodes (some of whom in the event were saved by the Turks). The Americans were not sorry to see this fiasco develop, as many of them resented Churchill's unwillingness to contemplate the cross-Channel invasion. Now, they produced a wrong-headed scheme of their own. Seven divisions were taken away from Italy, to launch an invasion of southern France when the time came. It was pointless, and the British in Italy could complain that they were too weak to do what they were supposed to do. The controversy on this goes on and on.

At Teheran, the communizing of eastern Europe was already implicit. It was happening not just through the Red Army but also through the resistance movements, which in most countries—though not Poland—were heavily influenced by Communists. Resistance in any advanced, urban country—France and the Czech lands the obvious cases—was best carried on, where at all, through sabotage, because random killing of this or that German invited gruesome reprisals. The Communists encouraged these, as it made the locals hate the Germans even more, and so swelled Communist ranks, but that was only really possible in countries such as Greece or Yugoslavia, where the partisans, supplied by air, could hold out in barren mountains. By 1943 resistance movements had grown, and collaborators disappeared as best they could: there were prominent defections from Vichy France. The Communists now controlled much, and in northern Italy were even set to take over when the Germans went. At Teheran it was agreed that Poland should be shifted to the west, losing roughly the same territories given to the USSR in the Molotov-Ribbentrop Pact, and being compensated in the west from German industry-rich territory; in time, five million Poles would be deported from east to west. The extension of Soviet influence to other lands became ever more likely, with Churchill's connivance. He went to Moscow in October 1944 and arranged the deal.

The British really wanted Greece for their key position in the eastern Mediterranean, with the Suez Canal and Middle Eastern oil in the offing. Stalin agreed to rein in the Greek Communists, who were slaughtered when they tried to take power at the end of the war. Stalin did nothing to help them. The counterpart was that Churchill wrote off the rest of the region, except for Yugoslavia, where he agreed on a half-and-half split of influence. Tito's Communist Yugoslav partisans were then given prodigious help by the British, whose Special Operations Executive (SOE) officers had the adventures of a lifetime in the Dalmatian karst (the novelist Evelyn Waugh, a Catholic, was there for military intelligence, and was repelled by the duplicity and cruelty he encountered, as shown in *Sword of Honour*, his great trilogy on the period. He had no illusions as to the collaboration of a part of the British establishment and the Yugoslav Communists, and it gave its fruits twice over—once when Stalin broke with Tito in 1948, and again when Yugoslavia eventually disintegrated in 1991: the Foreign Office gave sneaky support to the Serbs). But there were further gains for the Anglo-Americans, in that Stalin told the Communists in the French and Italian resistance not to seize power, whether in Paris or Milan, come liberation. They quite easily could have done. Stalin instead did a deal with the French leader, General Charles de Gaulle, whom he recognized before the Americans (who detested him). In the fullness of time, President de Gaulle was to weaken the Anglo-American financial and military system. In 1968 there was a rebellion in Paris against him, and the Communists could have toppled him, but Moscow again told them not to, because he was more useful to them than ever a Communist régime would have been. All of this was in the tea leaves at Teheran. There was one further British concession at this time, one that gave almost no cause for reflection. Hundreds of thousands of Soviet and Yugoslav citizens had volunteered for German service, in some cases to escape starvation. At the end of the war, the British handed them back to Stalin and Tito, to years of captivity or execution. Thirty years later, Alexander Solzhenitsyn told the world what had happened. In this matter, the Americans behaved humanely—agreeing to hand back the prisoners, but in practice letting them escape.

And now the war was being waged increasingly from Washington. The background was the convulsive change in the American war economy. The New Dealer approach worked, as it was to do in postwar Europe in the years of the Marshall Plan: a manager in a short-fuse bustle, not accepting excuses. By 1943, the mighty automobile companies had converted for aircraft, and in 1944 produced thirty times more aircraft than in 1939. In all, 50,000 bombers and 60,000 fighters were produced, to the Germans' 40,000 total, but the Americans produced spectacular improvements in quality—a fighter with the range for Berlin and back to England, and a B-29 bomber with much sophistication of navigation, speed, and bombing load. Some hundred shipyards had been subjected by outsiders to mass-production methods. American yards had produced seventy ships in all between 1930 and 1936, but now turned out 6,000 after 1942—twenty times more in 1944 than in 1940. These were ugly, short-lived Liberty ships (and the prototype was British), but they served their purpose. The results were shown on both of the world fronts on which Americans were active: aircraft carriers, elaborate bombers, eventually also atomic bombs.

A biblical fate awaited Japan, once the Americans could establish a proper base for the delivery of fire and brimstone. They were creeping towards one. On 15 June 1944, 535 ships began landing 128,000 US Army and Marine personnel on the island of Saipan, expecting to set up airfields for the B-29s to reach Tokyo. It was done in ninety days, and the Americans now had fifteen carriers, a thousand aircraft, seven battleships, and seventy destroyers, with much else, against nearly all of Japan's remaining fleet, nine carriers and five hundred planes. This force had lost almost all of its submarines, as the American destroyers benefited from much superior intelligence, and the Japanese land-based planes were similarly knocked out. The bulk of the Japanese army was not engaged against the Americans at all, but was scattered over the huge expanse of China, and, at that, involved in a large, successful but ultimately pointless offensive that was designed to knock China out of the war. Meanwhile, the British had at last defeated some of the Japanese army on the Indian border. In the other, not well coordinated, part of the American advance, MacArthur had cleared New Guinea and landed in Indonesia; he would soon land at Leyte, returning, as he had once promised, to the Philippines, where plenty of evidence came up in the atrocious Japanese treatment of native populations and prisoners of war. The way was open to a spectacular bitter end, when American bombers could devastate the Japanese mainland at will.

In the same fortnight as the invasion of Saipan, a vast force also struck in France. The Allies had taken their time, with endless meticulous preparation—nothing of the old British slapdashness. One of a few dozen Luftwaffe pilots, later a successful industrialist, described how, in the early hours of 6 June, he took his machine up for a patrol, and saw the invasion fleet, with its cloud of air cover—7,000 ships carrying 160,000 men with thousands of planes above them. He knew then that the war was lost, but meanwhile, using cloud cover, he knocked out six aircraft before fuel shortages forced him down. In the same way the once-formidable U-boats managed to sink only one ship, a Norwegian destroyer. The whole thing was presided over by a cunningly genial American, Dwight D. Eisenhower (the name is of German origin and means 'ironworker'). There were of course deep currents of resentment on both sides in the Anglo-American alliance, but Ike surfed them, and the British were sensible in not fighting, as weaker allies tend to do, for insignificant symbols of prestige. They did not on the whole believe in the invasion, but they went ahead. The Americans turned out to have been completely right, for the invasion was extraordinarily successful.

Looking back, we can see that the Normandy invasion should have been done in 1943. But initial plans were constricted by lack of landing craft, and also by the demands of the bomber offensive. In 1944, the planners elected not to attack an obviously defended seaport, and the short operating range of fighters limited the number of potential landing sites otherwise, in fact to two—Calais and the Normandy coast, where there was a port, Cherbourg, that could be taken from the side. Normandy was chosen and was carefully studied, the plan having been accepted by Roosevelt, Churchill, and Canadian PM Mackenzie King at the Quebec Conference in August 1943. Assembling the landing craft meant a delay till June, and the invading force was to number a million men. They gathered in the south of England. Preparation was very thorough, and even the nature of seaside sand was under review, so that in the peaty areas, tanks would roll out over a special matting. There were two artificial harbours for offloading cargo on the beaches of Normandy. They would be towed out in bits from England and assembled off the Normandy coast. An oil pipeline would be installed under the Channel. The Germans were completely fooled as to the direction of the attack, and every single German spy was identified and used, for purposes of deception. For a week, the Germans thought that the Normandy invasion was a feint, that the real one was coming at Calais. The task was formidable, as Rommel had organized the defences: there were steel traps at the high-tide level, thick bunkers, and, against aircraft, booby-trapped staves in fields; low-lying areas had been flooded. There was barbed wire everywhere. Four divisions were in the area, and there were of course Panzer divisions in reserve, though only one was in the Normandy region, and able to intervene on the first day. Preventing German movement of reserves was essential, because they could travel far faster by land than could Allied ones by sea (a single division needed forty standard-size commercial ships). That would mean watching the eastern flank of the invasion, on the Orne River, which flowed through Calvados and the town of Caen, and the British were to drop parachutists to secure the bridges to stop German armour, while the five designated beaches were attacked from the sea.

Surprise was total. Everything would depend on the moon, the tides, and the weather, and an invasion could only occur on a few days in every month. The weather was very bad on the day designated—5 June—and the Germans themselves rested, or in Rommel's case went to a birthday party. Then an ingenious weather expert allowed the huge force to lift off on 6 June, D-Day (the 'D' stands just for 'day', that is, the unspecified future day when a planned manoeuvre would commence). The airborne landings that preceded this worked, in the main, because they had been expertly prepared with mock-ups of the landing places. Cooperation of the French Resistance on the ground helped immensely. The initial landings also succeeded, though the Americans had a hard time at one of their beaches (Omaha) where they had high losses as they were fired at from heights, but small groups of infantry managed to get through the defences in the end. The British had few problems although they did not take Caen, an immediate objective. Once the beachhead was established, the artificial harbours were started, and moved 9,000 tons per day even after one of them was destroyed by an enormous storm on 19 June (showing what might have happened if such a storm had hit on the 6th). Casualties were lighter than expected (10,000, whereas Churchill had feared twice as many) and the bridgeheads held, perhaps not surprisingly given the ten-to-one air superiority and the sabotage of the railways by the *maquisards* (French Resistance). The local German reserve had met stiff resistance, and other reserve divisions were too far off—still held up by the illusion that a main attack was coming at Calais, anyway reduced to moving only at night, on bicycles.

The Allies faced a considerable task as they went inland. The Americans moved northwest and on 18 June took the port of Cherbourg, with a deep-water harbour, which was, however, in useless condition. The British (with Canadians, Poles, and others) had to go inland across very difficult terrain, the *bocage*, of high hedges and narrow roads, ideal for the defence. Montgomery, as commander of the mainly British (with Poles and Canadians) 21st Army Group, was put in overall charge of the invasion until the Americans were able to set up their own army group, called the 12th, under Bradley. Montgomery was unable to exploit the initial German weakness because of the great storm between 17 and 22 June, and the Germans at last built up strength around Caen. It was assaulted again and again, and did not fall until the end of July, in a condition of ruin. The point of Montgomery's strategy was to pin as much of the German army on this, the eastern side, so that the Americans, clearing the much more thinly defended western side, could finally outflank and envelop the Germans. This took time, but in the end Montgomery succeeded: there were seven Panzer divisions against him, and only two against the Americans. At the end of July, the Americans did get round the German western flank, and liberated Brittany. The German forces were being encircled south of Caen, and the generals wanted a retreat to the Seine.

Eisenhower was now supreme commander in the field and discharged his duties with great skill, particularly as regards the temperamental Montgomery.

Hitler was set on a great counter-attack. He was now hardly capable of rational thought. On 20 July, one of the senior officers had tried to kill him, in a staff hut at the Rastenburg headquarters. He had failed, but Hitler was shaken and, arms a-tremble, never really recovered. His doctor prescribed pills, which caused flatulence. Now, when generals came to confer, they had to go through a security machine, their pockets patted down, their revolvers deposited on a tray. Hitler's orders for Normandy were known to the Allies through the code-breakers, Allied command of the air was now total, and the German counter-attack failed. The Allies could now think of trapping vast numbers of Germans, and this was left to General George Patton to effect, moving nearly unopposed east and then north towards Alençon. The Germans were left in a pocket. They fought, kept open a way for some at the town of Falaise (birthplace of William the Conqueror, who in 1066 launched an invasion in the other direction), but lost 50,000 men as prisoners by 21 August. It was the decisive battle, and three days later, on 24 August, Paris was liberated. Now—unnecessarily—an Allied invasion of southern France occurred, met no resistance at all, and by September seven field armies, including the French, were more or less at the German border. They were well-supplied and had had since the breakout in July a great superiority in numbers and tanks of four to one. In aircraft the superiority was shattering. What now? The Allies had had 240,000 casualties, with 36,000 killed and 4,000 tanks knocked out, but the Germans in France lost 300,000, two-thirds of them prisoners, and of 2,000 tanks, only 120 came back over the Seine. The Luftwaffe had ceased to affect matters, as Germany had produced one-sixth as many planes as the Allies in the previous year.

There were still very substantial Allied forces in Italy, and Churchill wanted to use them more productively. Perhaps they could forestall the Russians advancing into Central Europe and contain the Communist threat in the Mediterranean generally. The campaign went slowly, with prima donna generals and an overall commander, Sir Harold Alexander, who suffered from excessive politeness; there were some oddities (the Germans employed Cossacks and a Turcoman division). The Allies assaulted the Gothic Line late in August, and in mid-September the plains of Lombardy were in sight, but then rain fell, with landslides and torrential rivers. Movement was desperately slow, the Germans stubbornly reorganized, Italian collaborationist forces still operated under the shadow Fascist régime that the Germans kept going for Mussolini on Lake Garda, and the partisans threatened to pre-empt Allied government. This went on until April 1945, when the German commanders negotiated a separate surrender ten days before the end, and Mussolini's corpse was famously hung upside-down outside a garage in Milan. The Italian partisans who killed him were Communist and would no doubt have taken power there and then, but Stalin was firm in his instructions to their leader, the grumbling Palmiro Togliatti: cooperate with the western Powers and their nominees. The British and the Russians now in effect moved into their separate parts of the

Balkans as the German Army Group E retreated towards Croatia and Trieste.

There had been an eastern equivalent to Germany's western collapse. The Red Army now had enormous weight to deploy. In coordination with the western Allies, it timed a huge offensive to go with the Normandy invasion, and called it Bagration, after a Russian general of the Napoleonic era. On 23 June the Red Army struck at Army Group Centre, which was in an exposed position, trying to hold the land bridge between the rivers, west of Smolensk, to keep open a link to Army Group North, under pressure in the Baltic. It had had to part with tanks and aircraft for the west and aircraft to defend the German cities. The Russians were now adept at what they called *maskirovka,* misleading the Germans with various tricks as to the weight and direction of their attacks; and there was in any event a serious threat to the German line in the south, as the Germans were forced to abandon Odessa, and Rumania herself came under threat. By late August, the pressure upon her was such that the king behaved as his Italian counterpart had done a year before, and arrested his equivalent of Mussolini, Marshal Ion Antonescu; Rumania then became a Soviet ally. Hitler underestimated the danger posed by Soviet troops facing Army Group Centre, which had sent a third of its guns and nearly all of its tanks to the south, where the attack was expected. The Panzer groups had done creditably, under Manstein, on the borders of Rumania, but had of course been diverted from the centre in the process. Four Soviet army groups were devoted to the operation, and there was a large concentration also against the Germans' North Ukraine

Army Group, to the south, where the main city of southeastern Poland, Lwów, was the target. The Russian partisans were blowing up railway tracks through the forests and attacking cut-off German units. Then 1,700,000 men, 24,000 guns, 4,000 tanks, and 6,000 aircraft went into action, against 800,000 men, 9,500 guns, 500 tanks, and 800 aircraft. The one German advantage lay in strong defensive lines, built up over time. The main offensive started on 23 June with a crushing bombardment, and the defences were nearly broken. On the northern side, the First Baltic Army Group crossed the Dvina and trapped a corps of 30,000 men on 25 June at Vitebsk, which fell two days later. The Third Belorussian Army Group drove through an army at Orsha on the Moscow-Minsk high road and reached the river Berezina, where Napoleon's army had had its most spectacular disaster in 1812. This also became a trap for two German corps, because, to the south, strong Russian forces crossed the Dniepr near Mogilev. By 27 June, the two German corps were encircled in a pocket east of Bobruysk, constantly bombed, and though part of the Ninth Army managed to escape, 70,000 troops were killed or captured. After that the Russians moved on Minsk itself, scene of their great disaster three years before. From 28 June, the Third Belorussian Army Group crossed the Berezina, and to the south the First Belorussian Army Group pushed another pincer. These forces met up in an encirclement west of Minsk, trapping the entire German Fourth Army on 4 July. Army Group Centre was destroyed, maybe the greatest ever defeat of the German army, which lost twenty-five divisions, some 300,000 men. In the few subsequent weeks, the Germans lost another 100,000 men. About 90,000, with twenty-two captured generals, including four corps commanders (one of whom had deserted his own headquarters), were now marched through the centre of Moscow as a sign of Stalin's triumph. Many were so scared that they lost control of their bowels, and the streets had to be specially cleaned. There was then, of all things, a German recovery.

The German side had one remarkable commander, Walter Model. He took over Army Group Centre after the defeat, replacing Ernst Busch, a pliant yes-man for Hitler. Model managed a miracle of scraping troops together from anywhere and everywhere and restoring the link to Army Group North, itself facing troubles in the Baltic. By the end of July, Riga in Latvia was holding out, and in August, the Germans were even able to counter-attack near Vilna, which had fallen on 8 July. There was a sad postscript to twenty years' Polish rule of that great historic city, the spiritual centre of the eastern Jews, and also of the Catholic baroque. Young Poles rose in revolt to seize it before the Russians arrived, were slaughtered by the Germans, and later by the Soviets, and were buried outside the great cemetery with crosses made of rusting iron bars. Meanwhile, an attack developed in the south, and Białystok, also the scene of earlier catastrophe, fell on 27 July, after two days of fighting; between 18 July and 2 August, Konstantin Rokossovsky moved on Warsaw, reaching the Bug on 21 July and seizing Vistula bridgeheads by 2 August.

Now came an uprising in Warsaw. The Polish resistance had had time to organize, and the Nazi occupation, ferocious to start with, had become lazy and neglectful—even, in some quarters, sympathetic to the Catholic Poles. The uprising seemed to make sense, in that the German army was packing its bags, and the Russians were almost in Praga, the Warsaw suburb on the east bank of the river Vistula. Taking the capital before they got there would have great symbolic power, as with de Gaulle's taking Paris before the Communists. But the Germans struck back, using Ukrainian and Baltic troops who hated the Poles, and, by dint of burning down a good third of the city, they crushed the rebellion and held on in Warsaw until January 1945. The Russians, arguing that they had outrun their supply lines, did nothing—and not only that, they refused to help British planes supply the Poles. The fact was that Stalin was quite happy for the Nazis to crush the Poles (as he had shown in 1940 and, massacring 15,000 Polish officers at Katyn and elsewhere, was even prepared to help out). The London Polish exile government was itself at fault, in that it overrated British strength and refused to concede any border change, whereas the Czechs made a deal with Moscow, handed over a province to the east, and gained in return a withdrawal of the Red Army as soon as Czechoslovakia was restored. That the country went Communist in 1948 was not as straightforward as was the process in Poland, where there was an occupation and a puppet government. At any rate the Warsaw uprising was crushed, and when the city was liberated, it consisted of miles and miles of burned-out wrecks and rubble, with only the foreign embassies on the Aleje Ujazdowskie and the Gestapo-occupied Hotel Bristol still intact. Some Polish intellectuals, seeing this wreckage, looked to the new barbarian power to the east for inspiration. Why were the barbarian Russians more successful than the civilized Poles?

Now the German allies dropped out. The young king of Rumania had got rid of his Fascists, and there was an armistice, followed by a Rumanian declaration of war on Germany. Bulgaria, in not dissimilar circumstances, found herself for a time simultaneously at war with everybody, but joined the Allies. An interesting case (as with Czechoslovakia) was Finland's. The Finns had maintained relations with Moscow all along, had been careful to limit their collaboration with Germany, and survived as neutrals. The Hungarians vainly tried for the same, but their élite was Anglophile and had not maintained any kind of link with Moscow. When their government tried to get out of the war, it was overthrown by an SS coup, and sadists and fools (the Crossed-Arrows) were installed in its place. The Russians now went on towards the Reich itself. The Third Belorussian Army Group (commanded by Ivan Chernyakhovsky) managed to invade East Prussia in November and wreaked vengeance on a German village (which became a showpiece of German propaganda on Soviet atrocities and inspired a resistance that was far tougher in the eastern parts of Germany than in the western ones). They paused, and then moved towards Königsberg and Memel in the southeast corner of the Baltic. Rokossovsky was set to seal off the whole of East Prussia, as he drove up from Warsaw towards Danzig. Panic now seized the German East.

WORLD WAR TWO

chapter nine | THE END

*preceding page: Soviet troops putting up flags on the
remnants of the statue on the Brandenburg Gate, 1945*
(Bettmann/Corbis)

A tremendous vise had now gripped both Germany and Japan: on the one side, pulverizing air attacks, which by December 1944 had destroyed the sources of energy and transport, and on the other, gathering armies and ships of vast power. It would have made sense, obviously, for their rulers to throw in the towel, but both countries were in the grip of fanatical illusion, in Japan that, never defeated, she would be saved by a miracle. The Germans fought on because they had been maddened by the endless bombing and knew only too well the fate that would be theirs once the Russian tidal wave reached the river Elbe. Right up to the end, lunatic loyalists reigned, and Hitler was having his brother-in-law shot for defeatism; when Japan finally surrendered, the words could not be found in the imperial form of the language to say, 'defeat' and 'surrender'. The emperor had to say that the war had not necessarily turned out to Japan's advantage.

Germany was still capable of desperate action and was given a respite in the last three months of 1944. One synthetic gasoline works still functioned, in Pomerania. The western Allies held a line more or less on the Rhine by October 1944 and were inching their way into Germany at Aachen and Strasbourg. Starving Holland was still under German control, and so were Denmark and Norway. Central Europe was still under Fascist governments, and in Zagreb, capital of Croatia—a place where you imagine Richard Wagner's *Götterdämmerung* as comic opera by Franz Lehár—a writer, Josip Horvat, published his diary of that period. He described the inane ways of the Independent State of Croatia, while the milk delivery of the German plenipotentiary (who had once been Austro-Hungarian representative at Brest-Litovsk in 1918) is cut off by the partisans, there is a lack of serviceable razors, and the skies are full of ingenious aircraft on their way to bomb Budapest, Vienna, Munich. Looking out over the wreckage of a Munich that he had known in his and its great days before 1914, the aged Richard Strauss, whose half-Jewish grandsons had survived the war in semi-exile at Garmisch-Partenkirchen, wrote *Metamorphosen,* a tone poem that could almost count as Germany's funeral music. There were other musical footnotes about another Richard, and other grandsons. The Wagner family had had good and close relations with Hitler all along. When they were teenagers and young men, Richard Wagner's grandsons, Wieland and Wolfgang, called Hitler 'Uncle Wolf.' (The two would revive the Bayreuth Festival of Wagner operas after the war.) The Wagners had given him, for his fiftieth birthday, in 1939, when things were humming along, the original manuscript score of Wagner's last music drama, *Parsifal*, Hitler's favorite of all Wagner's works. Now, six years later, they wanted it back, before the Russians got it, and Wieland went to Berlin and persuaded Hitler to give him the score.

Whether it is a myth or not that the great German and Austrian orchestras played Wagner at their final concerts, they did not need to: it was being put into practice, though in grotesque form. Hitler was not a very good Siegfried, and Eva Braun was no Brünnhilde. He had told her to stay for her safety in south Germany, but she managed to fly into Berlin just before the Russians got there, announcing that it would be a terrible shame if Adolf did not marry her after all this time: what *would* history think if she only counted as his mistress? The Third Reich thus ended with a sort of shot-gun wedding and then a mismanaged cremation.

The western campaign went with strange slowness, perhaps because everyone concerned except perhaps Montgomery understood instinctively that there was no point in heroism with the end in sight. An odd moment occurred at Arnhem in the Netherlands in September. On 17 September, a British parachute division landed there, trying to capture the bridges on the river system that had defeated the Spanish over three centuries before. They were unlucky, in that they struck a Panzer corps that was being reconstituted after Normandy. Walter Model, 'Hitler's fireman', as John Keegan calls him, was moved from the Eastern Front and held the Arnhem Bridge, which condemned the British to a stagnant winter, or at most to painful inching forward. From September to December another Allied thrust ground slowly forward, at Aachen and into the Hürtgen forest, again against Model, a vastly effective commander and also the rudest man in the German army. This cost the Allies 33,000 killed and incapacitated. Aachen fell, the first German town to do so, but it was all slow going, and Hitler began to hope that something could yet be achieved against opponents as clumsy as the Anglo-Americans appeared to be. Could he swoop and seize Antwerp, their port, and drive them out of Belgium? Would they then ask to join him in fighting the USSR, the ghostly proposition that had been there all along? In the circumstances, the counter-attack was a bravura performance. With the last strategic reserve of the army, and just as the Russians were closing on Budapest, Model launched an attack in that very area of southeastern Belgium where the Germans had done so spectacularly well almost five years before. Using captured vehicles and gasoline, as Rommel had done after the fall of Tobruk in 1942, the Germans managed to get some way forward. Too much was made of this, for if the Allies were not good at offensives, they could readily manage a defence, and once the weather cleared, airpower was enough against German troops mired in traffic jams. By Christmas 1944 the attack had run out of fuel and was called off on 8 January. Then there was more inching forward, and in mid-March Model was forced back when the Americans captured the Ludendorff railway bridge over the Rhine south of Cologne while the British and Canadians pushed on towards Hamburg. What was left of Model's army group was encircled in the Ruhr, and the question was whether the great industries would be destroyed, as Hitler wanted. Germans with foresight sabotaged the orders, and so did Model, but he would not surrender. He discharged the men, and shot himself.

The western Allies walked forward unopposed until, in a small Saxon town, they met up with the Russians, on 24 April. Next day, the event was staged again for the cameras at Torgau, where there was a bridge over the Elbe (ironically, the 'Torgauer Marsch' had been Hitler's signature tune). Later on there was some argument that the western Powers should have reached Berlin first. Why had they allowed Stalin to get there first? The argument really applies to what happened in 1943, when Churchill had been stuck in North Africa and Italy; and anyway the Russians themselves argued as to why they had not been the ones to reach the Ruhr, thereby securing the economic future of the Soviet Union, before the western Powers managed to seize that industrial blue chip of blue chips, which re-launched West Germany as a world-class economy in alliance with the North Atlantic Treaty Organization (NATO). Soviet generals, weighed down by advertisement-hoardings of medals after the war, argued that Stalin's fixation with the pockets left behind by Hitler on the Baltic, the largest of them in Latvia, had been responsible. However, the Germans were resisting with a madness in the east that can only be explained in terms of what they knew was coming.

Hitler had decreed that there should be no retreat. On the contrary the forces should stay where they were (*eingeigelt* or 'be-hedgehogged') as at the turn of 1941–42. Large parts of the Red Army were waylaid in the Baltic and East Prussia for a long time, and then there were the troubles in the south. Budapest was one of the great cities of Central Europe, and the Danube was the great obstacle to Soviet penetration. There was a six-week siege, and much of Buda was shattered in the Germans' last-ditch resistance, which collapsed in February. The news of Mussolini's death (he died April 28) reached Hitler just as the Russians arrived on the outskirts of Berlin. The Russians had concentrated, in the winter of 1944–45, on their Balkan front, and had cleared Belgrade in October. They had been held up by the forces that Hitler had left behind in the north, and they now needed to concentrate again for further advance in Poland. Another great Soviet attack rolled forward on the Vistula, again with much care taken for surprise to be total. Hitler had appointed Himmler to command the renamed army group in this area, and the Nazi Party's armed wing, the Waffen-SS, was now almost a million strong (it had many foreign volunteers), but there was no stopping the Red Army, which, moving twenty miles every day, broke into East Prussia, and even entered Elbing and Heiligenbeil when the trams were still running.

By 24 February all German counter-attacks had failed. The Russians stood on the river Oder, only fifty miles east of Berlin. Before them, they had driven hundreds of thousands of refugees, families with carts, plodding their way through the snow, desperate to reach the other bank of the Oder or the sea, across the frozen lagoons. There have been some classics of German literature on this subject. In *Recollections of an Old East Prussian,* Alexander Fürst zu Dohna-Schlobitten writes about how he had been allowed to fly out of Stalingrad because he had six children. When he got home, he led his estate workers away from the family's historic Schlobitten manor house to the west, with even a wobbling wheel being cause for wild alarm as they trekked through the forests to safety. *The Book of the Thuringian Nobility* by Adam von Watzdorf and others describes another trek, this time of British prisoners of war, marched away from a camp in Silesia, and fed hot potatoes by the estate owners as they passed through. Thousands of German civilians, military, and Nazi officials fleeing the Russians managed to pack themselves into a Baltic steamer, the *Wilhelm Guttlof*, which was sunk by a Russian submarine: 9,000 drowned in what counts as the worst maritime disaster, ever. By mid-March the Russians were in Silesia and Pomerania, had taken Zagreb, and were about to take Vienna (13 April). Meanwhile air raids went on and on against Berlin; the last, an RAF attack, was on Potsdam on 14 April, which destroyed the old Garrison Church and much else. The great effort to help the Russians occurred in mid-February, when the RAF destroyed Dresden, on account of its railway network (which recovered quickly). This episode became very contentious, Churchill himself protesting at the wreckage of 'Florence on the Elbe', though there was an element of hypocrisy to the objections, in that Churchill himself had been an ardent supporter of area bombing. As to Berlin, RAF Mosquitoes—fighter-bombers— kept bombing until Hitler's birthday on 20 April.

There are photographs of the Führer, now fifty-six but looking much older, patting the cheek of an adolescent boy in a greatcoat too big for him (an orphan from Dresden), as the boy joins the Volkssturm national territorial militia. On 9 April Königsberg, widely wrecked, gave in and Zhukov was able to concentrate on the last obstacle before Berlin, the Seelow Heights, while Rokossovsky's and Konev's army groups, to north and south, also concentrated against Berlin—altogether 2,500,000 men, 6,250 tanks, 7,500 aircraft, and over 40,000 guns (with truck-mounted Katyushas, each of which fired dozens of rockets). A ferocious last stand took place on the Heights, but by 19 April the defenders were again overwhelmed, and though the cost was high—30,000 dead and nearly 3,000 tanks lost—Berlin was encircled. On 22 April Hitler saw that his ideas for rescue from somewhere, Silesia or wherever, could not be realized, and he fell into that famous rage against his generals, which no one present forgot. He said he would stay in Berlin and commit suicide. Fifty thousand soldiers, 40,000 elderly territorials, teenage boys, and some foreign SS men (including two dozen British, a small Union Jack sewn onto their jacket-sleeve) fought on, while the inhabitants cowered where they could in a city under constant bombardment. Battles raged for the Havel bridges and along the main arteries of Berlin, towards the stations and the monuments, including the Reichstag. Bizarrely, the Victory Column, marking Bismarck's wars, was not knocked down, nor were the triumphalist busts of the worthy rulers of old Brandenburg, but the Russians were into the government quarter by the end of April.

Hitler staged his final scene: the wedding in the early hours of 30 April, complete with white-uniformed servants handing out open-faced sandwiches with *Sekt*, sparkling wine; the bystander hauled in from outside, who was able to perform the wedding ceremony because he was a civil servant, in his case deputy chief of rubbish collection for Pankow; his solemn question to the couple, 'Are you of Aryan origin?'; the vegetarian wedding breakfast; the suicide; the clumsy disposal of the remains, which ended up in boxes with other bits of bunker corpses, including a dog and its puppies on which the suicide pills were tested because no one trusted the SS doctors to supply proper cyanide (the dogs' trainer later went mad). When it was known that Hitler was dead, the secretaries and adjutants in the Chancellery put on jazz and lit cigarettes—forbidden in Hitler's presence. Hundreds of thousands of German prisoners marched off to the USSR, many never to return (and the bunker prisoners not until 1955, because they were tortured, the Soviet chief of security Lavrenty Beria not being sure that Hitler had not escaped). The final surrenders, one for the Allies, one for all forces, including the USSR, occurred on 8 and 9 May. A very tired Churchill was quite soon at the scene of the bunker, but the end of the Third Reich was not a moment for exultation, as the Armistice of 1918 had been. As many as 70 million had died, and Europe (and much of Asia) had been comprehensively wrecked. The strange thing was that, with all the fanaticism that had gone into the last stand, there was almost no subsequent resistance. The Germans had been deeply cowed, and when the newsreels of the concentration camps were (compulsorily) shown to them there were few attempts to justify them, and the only pseudo-serious attempts at revisionist history have come from Allied countries. In the immediate postwar years, twelve million Germans fled to the west, and perhaps a quarter of them died of exhaustion, starvation, illness, or violence, while harmless families who had never even voted Nazi were expelled from farms in the Czech lands or Silesia, after posters had gone up in public places, proclaiming, in words that the Nazis had used for the Jews, 'All Germans, regardless of age or sex, will assemble in the town square at . . .' for deportation, a suitcase each, to some ruin of a German town. It was, as was ruefully pointed out at the time, *Heim ins Reich*, 'Back home to Germany', and a much smaller

Germany. West Germany played a long game, of reconciliation, and that was, in the end, triumphantly successful.

It was a cause of very intense irritation to the Allies that the Japanese, seeing Hitler's end, did not take the point and give in. Saipan had cost the Americans an enormous effort, but their aircraft were now within reach of Japanese home territory. To the south, MacArthur was coming up to the Philippines again. In the latter part of 1944, the Americans were reaching places from where they could bomb Japanese cities. In the Battle of Leyte Gulf, off one of the Philippine islands in October, battleships of vast size had fought, and the Japanese had made devastating use of a new weapon, the suicide-bombing kamikaze aircraft, crashing on decks. Roosevelt had authorized MacArthur to concentrate on the Philippines, to cut Japanese supply lines, but Admiral Chester Nimitz had his own opinions and controlled the navy, sending the carriers against Formosa (now Taiwan). That move had the useful effect of drawing off Japanese planes, of which 600 were knocked out in three days, and there was therefore less Japanese air cover at Leyte Gulf. There was vast destruction of Japanese warships and carriers, and on 20 October the Americans landed on Leyte, more or less cleared it, and advanced on Luzon, the largest island of the Philippines, and towards Manila in January. A larger American force was used in this than in North Africa or Italy, and the fighting was particularly vicious, nearly all of the quarter-million Japanese defenders of Luzon being killed, though the remainder were still pointlessly fighting when the war stopped. One of the main Philippine islands, Mindanao, saw such resistance until August 15. Earlier in the year,

Anglo-Indian forces had liberated Burma, in Operation Dracula, a nocturnal and amphibious landing carried out with dash, though in fact the Japanese had just gone away. Some 150,000 Japanese died fighting in Burma with under 2,000 taken prisoner, only 400 of them touch-and-go healthy. If Japanese soldiers were going to behave in this way, then there could be no hope for a rational end to the war.

The southern Japanese home islands were now in the sights. There was Iwo Jima in February, and then Okinawa in May–June, where kamikaze suicide pilots caused the greatest losses ever suffered by the US Navy in a single battle, killing 5,000 men and sinking or damaging dozens of ships. Of the 117,000 Japanese troops tenaciously defending a very well-prepared Okinawa, nearly all died. It was an exercise in collective lunacy, and merely increased American determination to see the campaign through. Meanwhile, the Japanese war economy was collapsing. American submarines were now sinking the merchant fleet and would have done so entirely but they tended to be drawn off to sink warships instead. In October the Japanese had little petrol left, and their largest battleship, *Yamato*, when it set out for Okinawa, could only be given 400 tons, filling only a tenth of its petrol tanks. That blockade could of course have gone on, destroying the country without any need for a land invasion. But then there was the US Army Air Force, which promised decisive results from bombing. The American bomber, the B-29, had had its teething troubles. It was extremely sophisticated and had armour that machine-gun bullets could not pierce. But it took a year or so of accidents and faulty tactics before the plane could be properly used as, under Curtis LeMay, happened, once the airports at Guam had been properly set up.

How the Japanese had fought this war was now clear, as emaciated prisoners of war were freed, one third of their numbers having died (as against five percent of Americans and British in German hands). As the Philippines were liberated, there were massacres of despised locals, and in Singapore and Indonesia there had been brutal treatment of the natives, particularly the Chinese. The atrocities in China have been well-documented, and the figures for Chinese deaths can never be properly ascertained given the circumstances: estimates run from sixteen million to over twenty, almost as high as the Soviet ones, even then not including the losses of the 1930's, in which China was at war for most of the time. Meanwhile, there seemed to be no sign that the Japanese would recognize reality and give in. The three victors had met at Potsdam from 17 July to 2 August, and invited a Japanese surrender. With the end of the German war, the time had come for a concentration on the Pacific. When the three leaders had met at Yalta, in February 1945, a bargain had been struck, to the effect that when the war in Europe ended, the USSR would break the non-aggression agreement with Japan and declare war. In return Stalin was handed control of Europe east of the Elbe (and he understood it to mean gains in Iran and at Turkey's expense as well). The Americans did not of course want the Soviet Union in China, let alone Japan, but they did not want to have to reduce Japan on their own.

Stalin promised to act three months after the war ended in Europe and did so exactly on schedule on 9 August by invading

Manchuria. A million soldiers caused rapid collapse of the Japanese there, and a sign of what might have been expected had the war continued was that, in the chaos, plague-infected rats escaped, spreading an epidemic. But there was a far greater strike in this month. Strategic bombing, under LeMay, had become devastating. Japanese houses were small and flimsy, famously made of wood and paper, to offset earthquakes. As such, given the widespread hatred of the Japanese, they were obvious targets, and once the B-29s had solid airports and, at Iwo Jima and Okinawa, places in which to refuel or find repair, the cities of Japan became easy targets—the more so as they had nothing like the fighter and Flak protection that the Germans developed. Very few B-29s were knocked out by Japanese fire: the casualties were mechanical, or from the weather, and sometimes from pilot error. Japanese industrial production, anyway hit by blockade, spiralled down, and on 9–10 March 1945 alone, about 100,000 people were killed in a firestorm caused by an attack on Tokyo. Besides, the canals and rivers of Japan were mined from the air, in Operation Starvation, and Japanese families were not getting food. The same had happened in Germany.

Now began the final days of the Japanese Empire. The atomic bombs were dropped on 6 and 9 August. These had long origins, in good part Central European, and it was a curious retribution for the Nazi anti-Semitic campaign that talented physicists, some Jewish, ended up devising an atomic bomb. It was a triumph of British ingenuity and American enterprise as well. The Japanese still had links with Moscow and were trying to get the Russians to mediate and produce honourable peace terms, but they still made out that they were in a position of strength, infuriating their own ambassador to Moscow, a man of common sense. Meanwhile, the army chiefs in Tokyo talked serenely of resistance to the bitter end. In mid-July, the atomic bomb was successfully tested at Los Alamos in the desert of New Mexico. Harry Truman, now president after FDR's sudden death in April, was a scrupulous man, and did examine the question, as to whether dropping this bomb would be entirely moral, but he went ahead, and gave the Army Air Force a general authorization. Hiroshima had been left untouched, and on 6 August it was bombed and more or less flattened; 80,000 died. The Japanese went on wrangling among themselves, and another bomb was dropped on Nagasaki, killing 30,000 people. Still, the diehards tried to mount a coup, but they were beaten, and killed themselves. On 15 August the emperor, usually a symbolic figure, surrendered, on condition that his own role as guarantor of the permanency of Japan, would be respected. The Americans agreed, as they were already wondering how to treat Japan. With such dignity as could still be mustered, the old order in Japan presented itself on an American warship in Tokyo Bay on 2 September and signed an instrument of surrender, with General MacArthur looking triumphant.

Aftermath

World War One ended formally with peace treaties, the main ones drawn up within months of the Armistice. This was a mistake, because wartime hatreds were still poisoning the air, and the treaties negotiated in a vengeance-filled French capital did nothing to lessen the hatreds. The Germans were humiliated, and yet their new republic was required, by threat of starvation by blockade, to accept the terms; the republic was poisoned from the start. The war did not in fact end there and then with the Paris treaties. It went on and on—in Russia, where the Communists had won, and in Turkey, where the nationalists, with Communist help, defeated the western Allies, especially the British, and their proxies. It was in 1923, at the Treaty of Lausanne in Switzerland, that the war finally ended, and in 1924 there were at last serious moves to integrate Germany and her associates into a world system. The greatest German grievance concerned the indemnity which was supposed to be paid to the French and Belgians—reparations. All Germans blamed these for their economic troubles, the vast inflation especially. In 1924 a merry-go-round came into play, by which the United States lent Germany money to pay France, which could then pay its debts to Great Britain, which in turn paid its debts to the United States. This absurdity fell apart with the crash of Wall Street in 1929 and the subsequent disintegration of the international economy. Versailles and its codicils lasted for about a decade, and one sign that the French had given up on the whole structure was that in 1930 they began building the Maginot Line at huge expense (and thereby wrecked their defence effort with that gigantic white elephant).

The end of World War Two was even less neat than that of World War One. There was, in fact, no real German peace treaty for forty-six years, until 1991. An early attempt in the summer of 1944 was made at a German deal when the Big Three met at Potsdam, in a Sandringham-like residence that had been put up for the German crown prince in (of all dates) 1917. That meeting broke up without agreement on major matters, even on Germany's new borders in the east. In any case there was no German government with which negotiations might have gone on: the occupying powers simply argued among themselves, the French sometimes taking the Soviet side. The Cold War got under way not long afterwards, and maybe the best symbolic date to choose as its start is November 1945, when the Soviets refused to join in Anglo-American plans for the resuscitation of the world's economy.

One of the great differences between the two world wars is in the economic thinking that went on. Grotesque it now seems, but in 1918 the European capitals were full of plans to beggar neighbours. Georges-Henri Soutou in his 1989 book *L'or et le sang* made a long catalogue of these ponderings, and in the post-war settlement they came partly to fruition—new annexations, particularly in the Middle East; reparations to give German gold to France; confiscation of the German navy and merchant marine to favour the British; the Belgians even imagined that they should take over part of the Scheldt delta from the Dutch, to promote Antwerp's trade. The Americans were not greedy in these respects, but they were blind in another—wanting their dollars back from nations whom they were also preventing, via tariffs, from earning any. These nonsenses culminated in a world slump, which came back to haunt the United States with twenty-five million unemployed. After World War Two, wise men took the point of all this and said: Never again. When the British negotiated their wartime American loans, one of the clauses inevitably concerned the use to which the dollars would be put, and a great effort was made to pin the British down, to stop them from using American aid to promote their own trade with neutrals. Churchill was humiliated by the process. But out of it grew arrangements about monetary cooperation and Atlantic understanding as to what would have to be done after the war. Trade must never be allowed to collapse as it had done in the Thirties, with millions and millions out of work. There would have to be some sort of international arrangements to keep the money flowing to pay for trade, and that was arranged at Bretton Woods in the summer of 1944. This is the beginning of the International Monetary Fund and the World Bank, which came to the rescue of countries that might have brought down much of the world with them had they been allowed to collapse. The system did not work for some years after the war, because the Cold War broke out. One reason why it did not work was that, if countries wanted to benefit from Bretton Woods, they would have to lay their finances open to inspection, and the Soviet Union refused.

Germany now became the sticking point between the Russians and the West. The Russians wanted reparations and dismantled huge amounts of industry in the part of Germany they controlled. They also took captured rocket scientists who gave their secrets to the Soviet space programme (as of course happened with the Americans, though in this case the internees voluntarily cooperated and were well-rewarded). Germany beyond the Elbe remained in pitiable condition, a slave economy, and the concentration camps were kept going for recalcitrants. Moscow wanted the British especially to cooperate, as they controlled the Ruhr, the greatest industrial area (the American occupation zone, based in Frankfurt, was much less industrial). To begin with, British sympathies had been with the Russians; the British were responsible for all of northwestern Germany, which was in pitiable condition—mile upon mile of wrecked houses, canals, railways, factories. Millions of Germans had trekked from the east, and they competed for places to live, often little cairns of rubble, the inmates of which sold their bodies for cigarettes. Although the British were required, under agreements with the Russians, to send German machinery east as late as 1950, they knew that, if Germans were made to starve because of such reparations, the British and Americans would have to send food, even though it was running short in Great Britain. At first only very high-minded Americans and British objected to the terrible treatment of the Germans, but as the occupation went beyond the first months, that changed. CARE parcels flowed from the United Nations authority, and there was much private American concern as well (there was a specific collection for the Budapest intelligentsia, and it kept them going). There was of course a need for local government, and Germans could do the job better than untrained and ignorant Allied military; democratic-minded Germans who had been persecuted under the Nazis could be used to run it. Foremost among these was Konrad Adenauer, who would serve as West German chancellor, aged seventy-three to eighty-seven, from 1949 to 1963. Through the chaos of 1946, a new Germany was starting to emerge, and in September the American secretary of state, James Byrnes, made a famous speech at Stuttgart where he told the heads of the various German states, 'It is the view of the American government that the German people throughout Germany, under proper safeguards, should now be given the primary responsibility of running their own affairs.' The British and American zones were formally put together as the Bizone or Bizonia on 1 January 1947, allowing proper policies as regards transport and trade. Up to that point, German critics hyperbolically noted, the British occupation authority, with its socialistic attitudes (Labour's Clement Attlee had succeeded Churchill), was doing more damage to the economy of the Ruhr than the bombers had done.

Part of this story was just administrative improvements— necessity driving the Anglo-American authorities into cooperation with the Germans. But there was also the threat from the east. The Soviets did establish a democratic authority in Berlin right away, before the others: its nucleus was the group of German Communists who had lived through the war in Moscow, ruled by Walter Ulbricht. Stalin rather strangely expected that Germans would vote Communist, out of admiration for what he had achieved in the Soviet Union, defeating Hitler where the tsar had been defeated by the Germans. They did not—far from it. The standard answer to this conundrum was to compel the reigning Socialists to join up with the Communists and at Easter 1946, the Soviets bulldozed this through, by fear and blackmail. The Party of Socialist Unity emerged, Ulbricht with his irritating Saxon falsetto *Fistelstimme* in charge, to run East Germany with the usual fraudulent elections and dummy parties. On the other hand, at that time, at least minimal food was delivered to the population. In the west, by contrast, the months from January to April 1947, one of the worst winters ever, were marked by hunger and cold. Byrnes's successor as secretary of state, General George C. Marshall, travelled by train through a France on the verge of Communist takeover and through a wrecked Germany filled with wraiths to a Moscow that was grimly hostile. Stalin told Marshall he was confident that Communists would take over continental Europe, and as Lucius Clay, American deputy military governor, said, 'There is no choice between being a Communist on 1,500 calories a day and a believer in democracy on 1,000.' Stalin had already taken over Poland through fraudulent elections, and was soon to do so in Hungary and Czechoslovakia as well. In response in June 1947, at Harvard, Marshall announced that the United States would come to the rescue of western Europe. The then enormous sum of $5 billion was allocated to the relief of western Europe's immediate needs, which the exceptionally bad winter had made into a matter of life and death. Various institutions were set up to run the Marshall Plan, as even the French government had no idea about some of the vital statistics needed (and the Greek representative to the Marshall Plan's organisation for European economic cooperation was discovered in his Paris office making them up). The West Germans were now represented, their first appearance at the international level, though indirectly, through the American occupation authority. In the immediate moment, western Europe was indeed rescued, and the danger of Communist takeover, perfectly real in France, Italy, and Greece, receded. After that, the various states devoted Marshall money to their own needs, the Germans reconstructing their infrastructure and the British who, in 1946–47 had spent ninety percent of their own dollar earnings on cigarettes, mainly reconstructing their foreign investments (which recovered remarkably quickly, whereas British transport became the worst in Europe).

One thing the Americans did insist upon: that the Europeans should not just keep the money to themselves through control of money exchange; they should, by trade, spread it around. This meant that France and Belgium—then a considerable industrial power, with, as well, the resources of the Belgian Congo—should not discriminate against other countries, particularly Germany. Half of the Dutch economy had depended upon trade with Germany, the revival of which, in American eyes, was a prime necessity. Accordingly, a European Payments Union was set up to do for European trade what the IMF was supposed to do for world trade. In 1950, there was a strain on the new German currency, the Deutsche Mark, as Ruhr industrialists stocked up on raw materials to sustain the coming industrial export boom. The Payments Union took up the slack, and the Mark was saved. Curiously enough, in their anxiety to create a large European market on the same lines as their own, the Americans were first to propose a common European currency. The deputy head of the Marshall Plan suggested that it might be called the ECU, the European currency unit. Marshall money was subsequently rerouted into rearmament, at the time of the Korean War, but in these years the institutions of the postwar Atlantic world came into existence, one after and through another. There was the General Agreement on Tariffs and Trade (GATT) for freeing of trade in 1947, the OECD (Organisation for Economic Co-operation and Development, the Marshall office, still with us), the European Coal and Steel Community (ECSC) in 1951 to cartellize French and German coal and steel (the origin, if not of the European Union, at least of its flag, with blue for steel, black for coal, and yellow stars corresponding to the number of states involved, initially six). The whole was crowned by NATO, in 1949. Parallel with this came a Federal Republic of Germany, formally constituted in October 1949.

Postwar West Germany was a considerable success story. Germans had learned from the experience of Weimar. Its ponderously literal-minded constitution, providing for endless elections by proportional representation, had ended up with Hitler. The new Basic Law (in effect, the constitution) was short and to the point, with a good balance between centre and province, and protection for essentials, such as defence of the family against excessive taxation. The Federal Bank had instructions not to permit note inflation of the sort that Germans had twice experienced; a virtuous cycle of savings and investment got under way; and as early as 1955 German exports were greater than those of Great Britain, where the cycle was not so virtuous. Austria also became a model country. There was one admirable feature of postwar Germany, that, although the millions of refugees had had a horrible experience, with utterly innocent families being driven across borders with a battered suitcase, there was remarkably little complaint. The Sudeten Germans got on with their lives and made something of them. Germany's postwar leader, Konrad Adenauer, said that there would in the end be a magnet effect for the Communist East, and that was quite right, though the effect took longer than he expected. When the time came, the reconciliation of Poles and Czechs with Germans was quite painless. There was of course a cultural cost in all of this: a lack of national confidence, which was maybe the long-term effect of that terrible bombing. To echo A. J. P. Taylor: people no longer sang *Deutschland erwache,* but she had woken up just the same.

The story of postwar Japan is much like that of Germany. To start with, the American occupation had been very muddled, and Japan, like Germany, suffered two years of dreadful penury. Then, as with West Germany, administrative common sense, combined with a Communist victory, caused some rethinking. In 1949 the Communists won the Chinese civil war, and the defeated Kuomintang troops under Chiang Kai-shek retreated to the island of Formosa, Taiwan. The Americans then came up with a plan for the resuscitation of the Japanese economy, which turned into a stupendous success, as with West Germany. The economist Piero Sraffa, editor of the correspondence of David Ricardo and re-floater of Marx's sunken theory of surplus value, took two economic decisions in his life. He bought Japanese bonds in 1945, and he sold them in 1960 for gold, dying a very rich man (as Fellow of Trinity College, Cambridge, where he used to count the sugar lumps before his cleaning lady arrived and again after she left).

The contrast with the Communists became all too plain as the decades went by. The recovery of the USSR went ahead, partly through German slave labour (German prisoners built the Moscow skyscraper-cum-wedding-cake constructions). The extreme militarization, the ever-present secret police (eventually the KGB), and reparations goods from Germany allowed a recovery, although agriculture did not produce more than the tsars had done until 1960. Explosion of a Soviet atomic bomb was announced in 1949, and in 1950, when the Chinese went into Korea, the Cold War risked becoming hot. In fact the Korean War encouraged demand for raw materials, and for German machinery, and it caused the Western military-economic structure, NATO as its chief element, to harden and take effect. It lifted Germany in the 1950's and then Japan in the 1960's into positions of world wide importance. In time, this extraordinary and paradoxical development was to affect the Communist states. China, faced with the huge success, not just of Japan, but of

Taiwan and of South Korea, which in 1960 had exported only wigs, adapted her ways. Her success prompted the same in the USSR, which then disintegrated. At that, at last, a peace treaty was signed with a united Germany, and World War Two, forty-six years after the Allied victory, came to a formal end.

Political Boundaries in 1923

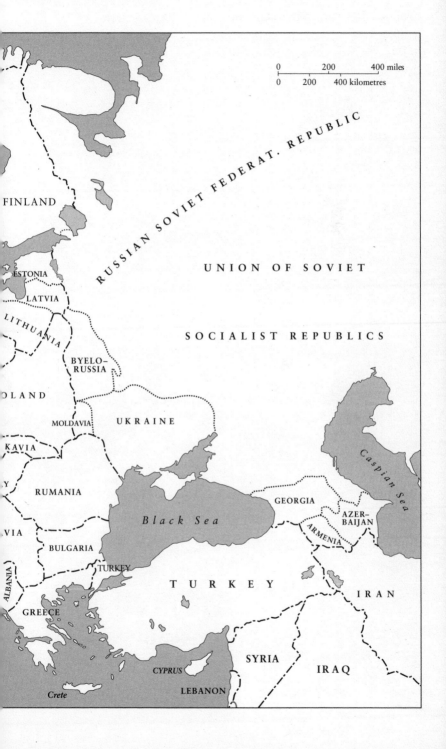

FINLAND

RUSSIAN SOVIET FEDERAT. REPUBLIC

UNION OF SOVIET

SOCIALIST REPUBLICS

ESTONIA

LATVIA

LITHUANIA

BYELO-
RUSSIA

OLAND

MOLDAVIA

UKRAINE

KAVIA

RUMANIA

VIA

BULGARIA

ALBANIA

TURKEY

GREECE

TURKEY

GEORGIA

ARMENIA

AZER-
BAIJAN

Caspian Sea

Black Sea

IRAN

CYPRUS

SYRIA

IRAQ

LEBANON

Crete

0   200   400 miles

0   200   400 kilometres

The Nazi Empire at Its Maximum Extent, Autumn 1942

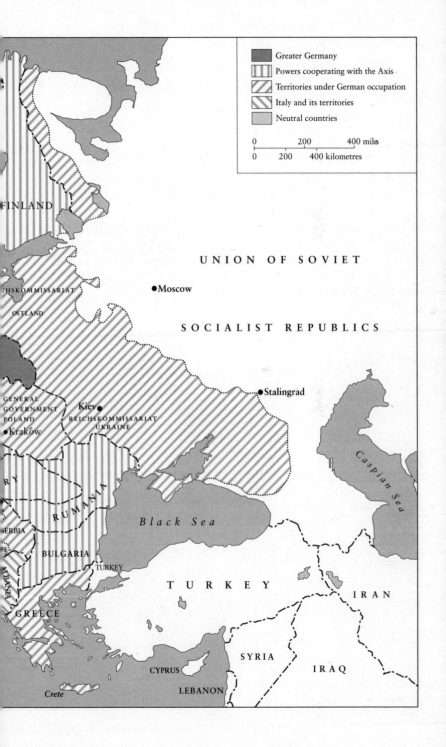

Greater Germany
Powers cooperating with the Axis
Territories under German occupation
Italy and its territories
Neutral countries

| 0 | 200 | 400 miles |
| 0 | 200 | 400 kilometres |

FINLAND

UNION   OF   SOVIET

●Moscow

.HSKOMMISSARIAT

OSTLAND

SOCIALIST   REPUBLICS

●Stalingrad

GENERAL
GOVERNMENT
POLAND
●Kraków

Kiev●
REICHSKOMMISSARIAT
UKRAINE

Caspian Sea

RY

RUMANIA

SERBIA

Black Sea

BULGARIA

TURKEY

TE

ΒΑΝΙΑ

GREECE

TURKEY

IRAN

SYRIA

CYPRUS

IRAQ

Crete

LEBANON

World War Two in Asia and the Pacific, 1941–45

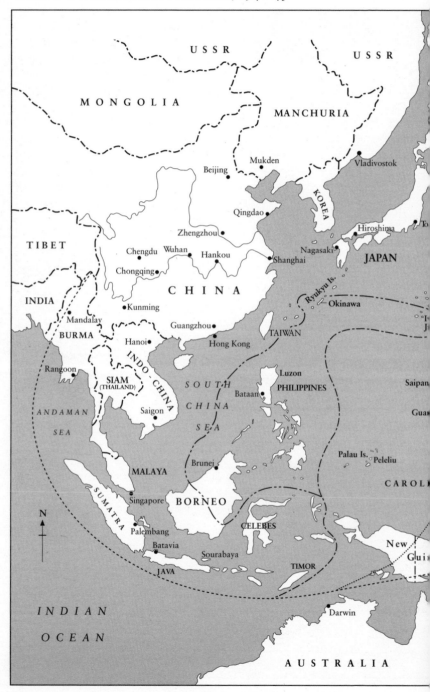

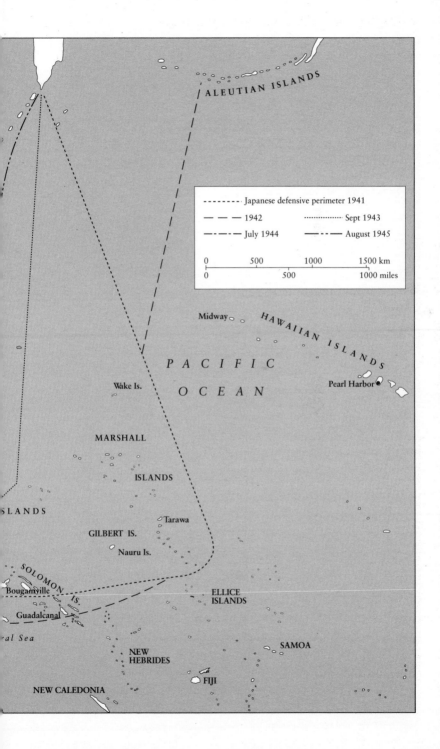

-----------	Japanese defensive perimeter 1941
— — —	1942
················	Sept 1943
—·—·—	July 1944
—··—··—	August 1945

0	500	1000	1500 km
0		500	1000 miles

ALEUTIAN ISLANDS

Midway

HAWAIIAN ISLANDS

Wake Is.

PACIFIC

OCEAN

Pearl Harbor

MARSHALL

ISLANDS

Tarawa

ISLANDS

GILBERT IS.

Nauru Is.

SOLOMON IS.

Bougainville

Guadalcanal

ELLICE
ISLANDS

al Sea

SAMOA

NEW
HEBRIDES

FIJI

NEW CALEDONIA

Acknowledgements

Over the years I have built up a good collection of books on the Second World War, my earliest purchases being A.J.P. Taylor's *The Origins of the Second World War* (1961) and Correlli Barnett's *Desert Generals* (1962). I have been lucky in being able to use excellent libraries to supplement this. The Bilkent Library, in the middle of Anatolia, has been built up in a relatively short space of time and is now remarkably useful; in England the London Library and Cambridge University Library are easy, agreeable, and endlessly rewarding: I am grateful to the librarians of all three. I am as ever grateful to my departmental head, Dr Pinar Bilgin, and to my other colleagues at Bilkent University for the happy and productive atmosphere they have created. I have also been fortunate with my publishers: Lara Heimert at Basic Books and Simon Winder at Penguin, and I am particularly grateful to my very genial and well-informed editor, Norman MacAfee. My son, Rupert Stone, has been my first reader, and I am glad to have had his encouragement.

Some Sources

There have been many and varied, and sometimes splendid, books on the Second World War, but my own preference is John Keegan's *The Second World War* (1990). It explains military technicalities, such as tank or aircraft design, very clearly and gives excellent short accounts of the various battles on land, at sea, and in the air. Any source list can only be a thimble in an ocean, and Keegan deals with the problem by confining himself to fifty books, most of which would be my own choice, and the best way forward is for me to offer a further fifty, published since then. This limitation is easier than it might have been, because English-language books, given the spread of the Internet and automatic translation, are overwhelmingly preponderant, far more so than in the case of the First World War.

The overall landmark history is now the thirteen-volume *Das Deutsche Reich und der Zweite Weltkrieg*, originally published by the Militärgeschichtliche(s) Forschungsamt (Freiburg-Potsdam) and in translation by Oxford University Press since 1990 as *Germany and the Second World War*. Its scholarship and fair-mindedness are above reproach. Michael Burleigh: *Moral Combat: A History of World War II* (2010) is a widening and deepening of an old classic, John Lukács: *The Last European War* (1976) and cf. Lukács's *The Hitler of History* (1997) and *The Duel* (2001), which is about the personal collision of Churchill and Hitler in the summer of 1940. The outstanding biography of Hitler is by Ian Kershaw: *Hitler* (2 vols. respectively *Hubris*—1998 and *Nemesis*—2000). There is hardly a topic, military or political, on which the author is not an authority, as I found when, as expert witness, I went through some of the sources in preparation for *The Guardian*'s court case against David Irving. Irving's *Hitler's War* (1977) could and should have been an outstanding book, especially on the run-up to Stalingrad, but was wrecked by the claim that Hitler did not know what was happening to the Jews. Kershaw's *Fatal Choices* (2008) concerns major strategic decisions. Gerhard Weinberg: *A World at Arms* (2005) is comprehensive.

On the origins of the war, A.J.P.Taylor's *The Origins of the Second World War* (1961) is still hugely valuable, the first hundred or so pages especially, in showing the weaknesses, sometimes ridiculous, of the Versailles order. Zara Steiner: *The Lights That Failed* (2005) is authoritative on the period up to 1933, when that order fell apart, starting with the world economy, and is more forgiving than Taylor. Antony Beevor: *The Battle for Spain* (2006) is very sophisticated, with much material on Communist hidden involvement in the Spanish Civil War. David Faber: *Munich* (2008) and Jonathan Haslam: *Russia's Cold War* (2011) deserve mention.

The campaigns of 1939–41 are covered in Julian Jackson: *The Fall of France* (2003), Karl-Heinz Frieser: *The Blitzkrieg Legend* (2005), and James Holland: *The Battle of Britain* (2010). The mobilization of the British war economy is well summarized in David Edgerton: *Britain's War Machine* (2011) but there is timeless interest in Correlli Barnett: *Audit of War* (1986), a memorable challenge to British smugness. His old classic, *The Desert Generals* (1960) on the North African war is also still very challenging. On the start and continuation of the bombing campaign over Germany, Max Hastings: *Bomber Command* (1976) is still the best. Robert Skidelsky: *John Maynard Keynes: Fighting for Freedom* (2001) is the established classic, wonderful in its understanding of wartime finance and the conditions in which the Treasury survived.

For the run-up to Barbarossa in 1941 see Gabriel Gorodetsky: *Grand Delusion: Stalin and the German Invasion of Russia* (1999) and Konstantin Pleshakov: *Stalin's Folly: The Secret History of the German Invasion of Russia* (2005). The Eastern Front has received a great deal of attention since 1989, as new documentation has emerged in quantities. Chris Bellamy: *Absolute War: Soviet Russia in the Second World War* (2007) is the overall authoritative work, but David Glantz also has a number of works that incorporate his own remarkable intuitions as to the *non-dits* of the Soviet official history: *The Gates of Stalingrad: Soviet-German Combat Operations, April–August 1942* (with Jonathan M. House) and *Armageddon in Stalingrad: September–November 1942* (2009). Glantz explained himself in an essay, 'Forgotten Battles of the Soviet-German

War, 1941–45' in Ljubica Erickson and Mark Erickson (ed.): *Russia: War, Peace and Diplomacy* (2004), which also contains important articles on aspects of the Eastern Front. Richard Overy: *Russia's War* (1997) is an older account, and the outstanding battle book is Antony Beevor: *Stalingrad* (1998). He explains the nature of his research—forbidding—in his contribution to the Erickson volume ('Stalingrad and Researching the Experience of War').

On aspects of Nazi rule in Europe and the western USSR, see Mark Mazower: *Hitler's Empire: Nazi Rule in Occupied Europe* (2008), which takes the place of the established Alexander Dallin: *German Rule in Russia 1941–1945* (1981). Christopher Browning 'Hitler and the Euphoria of Victory' in David Cesarani (ed.): *The Final Solution: Origin and Implementation* (1996) is the authoritative piece, but I still find the tone of Gerald Reitlinger: *The Final Solution* (1953) most appropriate. Since the Communist archives opened up, there has been careful work on Auschwitz by J.-C. Pressac: *Auschwitz* (1989) that supplies reliable statistics and tells the history of the museum (parts of which are reconstruction); see Hans Mommsen: *The Third Reich Between Vision and Reality* (2001) for an exposition of this author's varied explanations. Adam Tooze: *The Wages of Destruction* (2006) made waves as regards the crash of the German economy, which he makes out to have been much more militarized than we had supposed. Mungo Melvin: *Manstein* (2010) and Brigitte Hamann: *Winifred Wagner: A Life at the Heart of Hitler's Bayreuth*, 2007 are revealing miniatures.

In the end it was preferable that half of Europe would be under a Communism that might get better than that all Europe would be under a Hitler who could only get worse. But the latter stages of the war were dominated by the imminent handing over of Central Europe to Stalin: see Krisztián Ungváry: *Battle for Budapest* (2005) or Hans Graf von Lehndorff: *Ostpreussisches Tagebuch* (1985) and compare Alexander Fürst zu Dohna-Schlobitten: *Erinnerungen eines alten Ostpreussen* (1989). Götz Aly: *Hitlers Volksstaat* (2005) and Joachim Fest: *Staatsstreich* (1994) and *Der Untergang* (2004) are good German contributions, on the bomb plot and the bunker respectively. Jörg Friedrich: *Der Brand* (2002) saw the bombing from a German perspective.

The shaping of strategy in the western war is wonderfully described by Andrew Roberts: *Masters and Commanders* (2008) and compare Max Hastings: *Churchill: Finest Years* (2009). Carlo d'Este: *World War Two in the Mediterranean, 1942–1945* (1990), Rick Atkinson: *An Army at Dawn* (2002) on Torch, Niall Barr: *Pendulum of War* (2005) on the three Alamein battles, and Lord Carver: *The Imperial War Museum Book of the War in Italy* (2001) can be recommended. Allan Mallinson: *The Making of the British Army* puts these battles in perspective. Max Hastings: *Armageddon* (2004) is a good description of the end of the German war

On the Far Eastern war, see William B. Hopkins: *The Pacific War* (2010), John Toland: *The Rising Sun* (1970), Ronald Spector: *Eagle Against the Sun* (1985), and Max Hastings: *Nemesis* (2007).

Index

Soviet Union *(continued)*
  and Manchuria, invasion
    of, 186–187
  and Nazi Germany's final
    days, 181–182
  and Nazi Germany's final
    resistance, 179–180
  and Operation Bagration,
    167–171
  and Poland, 19–21
  post-World War II, 200
  POWs, German, 183
  and rail system, 68
  and U.S. Lend-Lease, 77
  and Yalta conference, 186
  See also Allies; *armed
    forces of;* Russia; Stalin
Soviet Union, Nazi Germany
  invasion of, 50–51,
    54–69, 95–111
  145–150
  and Battle of Kursk,
    144–149
  casualties, 64, 95, 98, 103,
    145
  and Crimea, 98
  and crisis of USSR in
    1942, 101–102
  and German retreat,
    149–150
  and Leningrad, 64–65,
    97–98, 110–111
  and Moscow, 63–64, 65–
    68, 97, 100–101
  and oil supply, 102–103

  and Operation Citadel,
    145–149
  POWs, Soviet, 138
  and Red Army,
    demoralisation of,
    101–102
  and Soviet rivers, 98–100
  and Stalingrad, 100,
    103–108, 115
  and winter warfare, 57,
    67–69, 97
  See also Red Army; Stalin
Space programme, 194
Spanish civil war, 10
Speer, Albert, xxiii–xxiv, 13,
    22, 119, 137
Sraffa, Piero, 200
SS, 10, 138
Stalin, Joseph
  and Berlin, 179
  and British spy, 146
  and Churchill, 115
  and Communist threat,
    post-World War II, 196
  and final war strategy,
    153, 158, 159
  and France, desire to
    invade, 115–116
  and Hitler, deal between,
    50–51
  and Hitler, trust in, 58
  and Italy, 166
  and military conspiracy,
    fear of, 50
  and Moscow, 66, 100–101

Vlasov, Andrey, 98
Voznesensky, N. A., 62

Wagner, Richard, 176–177
Wake Island, 74, 76, 77, 123
Wannsee conference, 139–140
War economy
  British, 120
  German, 96, 120–121,
    136–138, 145
  U.S., 159
War of Illusions, xv
Warfare. *See* Air warfare;
  individual armed forces;
  individual battles,
  invasions, operations;
  Sea power; Weaponry;
  World War I; World
  War II
Warsaw, Polish resistance in,
  169–171
Warsaw Ghetto, 151 (photo)
Warships
  British, xiv–xv, 75, 81
  German, xiv–xv, 31, 41
  Japanese, 184
  U.S., 44, 126
  See also Ships
Watzdorf, Adam von, 180
Waugh, Evelyn, 158
Weaponry, 79. *See also* Air
  warfare; Atomic bomb;
  Bombers; Battleships;
  Guns; *individual armed
  forces;* Sea power;
  Tanks

Weichs, Maximilian von, 109
Wells, H. G., xii
Wilhelm II, xiii
William of Orange, 116
William the Conqueror, 165
Wilson, Woodrow, 1
  (photo)
  and Treaty of Versailles,
    4, 5
Winter warfare, 57, 67–69,
  97
World Bank, 193
World financial crisis of
  1929, 7–8
World War I, 44
  and appeasement policy,
    10–11, 13, 16–17
  end of, 3–6
  illusions about, xv–xvi
  peace treaties, xvi–xviii,
    191
  reasons for, xiii–xvi
  and Treaty of Versailles,
    4–6
World War I, post-
  economic concerns,
    192–193
  reparations, 191–192
World War II
  Asia and the Pacific,
    206–207 (map)
  peace treaty, 1991, 192,
    201
  reasons for, xiii, xx–xxii
  See also Air warfare;
    individual armed forces;